D0104500

THE FEAST OF JOY

THE FEAST OF JOY

The Lord's Supper
in Free Churches

Keith Watkins

The Bethany Press
St. Louis, Missouri

Library of Congress Cataloging in Publication Data
Watkins, Keith
    The Feast of Joy
    1. Lord's Supper. I. Title.
BV825.2. W29   265'.3   77-525
ISBN: 0-8272-1006-X

Photographs on page 91, *Religious News Service,* page 13, Rohn Engh

Distributed in Canada by the G. R. Welch Company, Ltd., Toronto, Ontario, Canada.

Printed in the United States of America

To the memory of faithful persons who
as elders in the Christian Church
have represented this office at its best;
and especially
Martin Kullowatz of Portland, Oregon
Carl Albaugh and Chauncey Kessler of Somerset,
    Indiana
Paul Salmon of Fillmore, Indiana
Doyle Zaring of Indianapolis.

Having joined the twenty-four elders they say
with a loud voice:
"Worthy is the Lamb who was slain,
to receive power and wealth and wisdom
and might and honor and glory and blessing!"

Table of Contents

Introduction

The major act of Christian worship is a meal, a feast of joy where Jesus is the host and his people everywhere the guests. When the church first began, this table fellowship was the focus of their life together. Through later generations, while theologies have become elaborate and church life has assumed new forms, the Lord's Supper has remained. In our own time this ceremonial meal continues to be the most important form of worship offered up to God by those who trust in Jesus.

When I started this book, I had a very limited goal in mind: to prepare a manual of practice for ministers and elders in churches of the free tradition. I had intended to describe these leaders of worship and interpret the nature of their work, present a functional interpretation of their responsibilities, and supply prayers and other materials of worship suitable for use in the service of the Lord's Supper.

Yet in order to accomplish that first intention, I have found myself doing more. This book has become an interpretation of the meaning and character of the Lord's Supper. It is a personal statement growing out of my own experience and reflection—more a testimony than a definition. For more than thirty years I have been at the communion table nearly every Sunday, most of the time in congregations of the Christian Church (Disciples of Christ), as communicant, as minister, as Disciple elder. For half of that time I have been a seminary teacher, working with students preparing for the ministry in some two dozen church bodies. I have participated in ecumenical conferences, worshipped in many churches other than my own, read articles and books about worship and the Lord's Supper, published my ideas, and talked with many people. What follows has grown out of these experiences. I offer it in the hope that it will lead to the strengthening of the Lord's Supper in churches like my own and that it will be useful to people in other church bodies who want to learn from the experience of Disciples.

I am grateful for the help given me. Through the years my life has been enriched by the work of ministers and elders in churches where I have worshipped. At Christian Theological Seminary my colleagues on the faculty and students with whom I have worked have supported my labors, both by challenging some of my ideas and coming to agree with others. In the process of this interaction I have changed.

The writings of several scholars have influenced me greatly. Recently I reread Gregory Dix's *Shape of the Liturgy* and was surprised to find how much his exposition has formed my ideas about worship. The writings of Ernst Cassirer and Susanne Langer continue to shape my understanding of the nature of religious symbolic action. Victor Turner's expositions of how ritual works and what it accomplishes have helped me make sense out of many things that I could otherwise not understand. Among commentaries on the Bible that I have consulted in connection with portions of this book are works by Raymond Brown, Hans Conzelman, Martin Dibelius, and Artur Weiser. New liturgies, especially Presbyterian, Lutheran, Episcopal, and those of the Consultation on Church Union, have been constant companions. Horton Davies' five volume *History of Worship and Theology in England* has helped me keep historical truth in mind.

I happily confess my debt to Sherman Hanson and his associates at the Bethany Press. From the very beginning of this project, he has encouraged and cajoled me into doing more than I had intended.

Keith Watkins
Pentecost Season 1976

PART ONE

Festivals of Food and Light

A cake with one candle burning is set on the high chair with a flourish. While the parents and grandparents know the meaning of this event, the guest of honor is attracted not by meaning but by the brightness of the flame, the feeling of frosting squeezed between fingers, and the aura of excitement that surrounds the high chair. The happy birthday song, although sung vigorously, is scarcely heard by the child. Before the infant can burn a finger, the candle is blown out, the cake is cut, and the party continues. There will be many more birthdays, with growing depth of understanding, but perhaps none will carry that same kind of delight.

This birthday party is first for the parents as well as for their child. Through their earlier years they were formed by their parents, their ideas shaped, and their virtues developed. They were carried to events, held on shoulders during parades, sat on laps in church, feted at parties and family festivals. But now these two people, who had been the recipients of rituals of love and incorporation, are the conductors of them. They are now doing for the new generation what once was done for them.

The birthday celebration revolves around a highly structured ritual act. Invariably there is a cake. Candles, usually equivalent in number to the years of life, are lighted. A song known by everyone is sung. The candles are blown out, if possible with one burst of breath. The familiarity of the ritual is important. Because everyone knows it, everyone can participate. It is the same for child and adult, for laborer and aristocrat. Each successive repetition has its own importance but quickly fades into a montage of recollections in which the totality of birthdays is more important than any one party. It stays the same, which means that parents and children and grandparents are united in the same fabric of experience. Because each one goes through the same series of life stages, their separate life courses are blended into one human reality.

Several important values and sentiments are expressed in the birth-anniversary festival meal. Probably the most prominent of these meanings is the positive evaluation of growth and maturation. Especially during the first 30 years of life and in the years past 70, growing older is seen as an achievement to be applauded, and the birthday festival does so. A second meaning expressed is the solidarity of the family or circle of intimate friends. The birthday celebration brings them together in a way that exults in their mutuality of life. Although less clearly expressed, perhaps the most important of the values of the birthday party is the affirmation of personal worth. It provides an occasion for stating that the one being celebrated is distinct and worthy, desirable and wanted.

Because the birthday celebration is a festival, it takes on certain qualities. There is a kind of extravagance. If nothing else, the cake is cut more generously than on ordinary occasions. There are gifts and the expressions of affection are exuberant. Normal rules are momentarily suspended. People forget about their diets. The honoree is excused from normal chores such as helping with the dishes. The highly patterned, productive expectations are modified for the moment. People relax in the spirit of the occasion.

Of course, people can express all of these meanings without the traditional birthday party. Instead of a cake, there can be a pumpkin pie; no birthday song, no presents. The anniversary of the birth can be replaced by some other kind of date as the occasion for remembrance, perhaps the day of the person's patron saint as is the custom in some traditions. It is possible to express love and joy and individual uniqueness from time to time without special ceremony. Yet it is unlikely that these departures from custom will be exercised except on rare occasions, for however nonsensical birthday celebrations may seem to be, we enjoy them and we understand the complex pattern of meaning which this simple ritual of food and light expresses.

It is difficult to know what to call this cake and candle ceremony. Is it a party? A feast? A festival? A celebration? Each of these words suggests part of its meaning; yet each also conveys intentions quite different from those of the birthday ritual. All four words convey the sense of exuberance, delight, joy. Party and feast both imply that there will be food, although in a feast the meal is the center of attention whereas in a party it ordinarily is a subsidiary element. Festival suggests parades and a cluster of other events. Celebration implies grand style of performance, eulogy, and vigorous participation. A birthday in its broader form carries all of these qualities. Yet in its more specific form, a birthday gathering selects only aspects of each—the focusing function of food, the delight of celebrations, the giving of gifts which suggests the festival character of the event—and uses these aspects to express its own unique intentions.

The birthday celebration and the Lord's Supper are very much alike in that each uses a symbolic meal to convey complex and significant meanings. And it is hard to know what to call the Lord's Supper. Is it feast, which implies too much food? Or is it party, which softens the emphasis on food but implies too much concerning the supporting pattern of activity? Festival suggests exuberance, yet it says too much concerning a diversity of activities and the sheer fun of carnivals and fairs. Celebration avoids some of these other problems, but at the same time says very little about the nature of the ceremony. Feast is probably the best of these options. It implies food, exuberance, joy, style, all of which are important for the conducting of the Lord's Supper.

By comparing the service of communion with a birthday party, I have tried to suggest the general nature of the symbolism of this central act of Christian worship. I now want to move from illustration and suggestion to a more specific description of the Lord's Supper, stating what it means to call this act a *feast* and what is meant by the word *joy*.

The basic ritual symbol is a meal, one of the most necessary and natural human functions. We have to eat in order to live, and while we can consume our food in private, we much prefer to do so in company with others who also are eating. Because eating is so basic to human existence, and so universal, its mechanisms are known by all. We can manipulate knife and fork, or chopsticks, without thinking about what we are doing, and we can move the cup to our lips surely and gracefully. Chewing and swallowing take care of themselves. We can therefore move past the obvious purpose of a meal, which is to take in enough calories to keep life going, and focus upon other purposes that easily cluster around a meal. Eating and drinking together become the means of expressing friendship, showing the nature of marriage, demonstrating trust, extending hospitality, remembering past experiences.

As the name itself makes plain, the Lord's Supper is a meal. Its ingredients are simple. The one thing eaten is bread, a food that is virtually universal and available in countless forms. Grain is crushed into flour and transformed into something that provides many of the necessities for the sustenance of life. Grapes are crushed to provide the meal's drink, resulting in a beverage that pleases the tongue and brings delight to those who share in the meal. There has been an odd process of development in the character of these foods as used in the feast of joy. At first, the bread was leavened and the wine fermented, and the meal included other foods. In the apostolic age the additional items were dropped, and bread and wine were retained. A thousand years later, the church in Europe began to use unleavened bread. Although it still used fermented wine, it ordinarily permitted only the priests to drink from the cup during communion. In nineteenth century America, some protestants began using unfermented grape juice, and their descendants continue that practice. Yet whether leavened or unleavened, fermented or unfermented, the meal today continues to be some kind of bread, usually made from wheat, and squeezings from the grape.

When eating becomes a ritual, however, the primary purpose of eating is superceded by the special meaning, and in order to make that new meaning clearer and more forceful, the meal takes on a highly stylized form. For the birthday party, there is a certain kind of food, the cake, and specific ceremonies and songs.

17

For the wedding reception the menu and ceremonies are prescribed by custom. For the Hebrew religious meal there were specific prayers and ceremonies prescribed at the beginning and end of the meal. As the accounts of the Last Supper make plain, Jesus followed that same pattern when he ate with his disciples. He took bread, blessed, and distributed it before supper, and in similar fashion cared for a cup of wine following the meal. These prayers and ceremonies signalled that this meal was for more than nourishment and helped to express the added religious meaning.

There came a time, probably before the close of the New Testament period, when the meal became even more highly stylized. The natural side of it, the eating and drinking, was suppressed in order to let the new meaning be expressed without confusion or possible misunderstanding. People ceased to eat the full meal and instead partook only of the bread and wine used in the ritual of remembrance and praise. Once abridged and concentrated, the Lord's Supper remained a ceremonial meal rather than again becoming the full meal of meat and vegetables. Since then its purpose for Christians has been not the satisfaction of hunger but the expression of meaning. Because a normal meal is a time for eating, we want short prayers and minimal extraneous ceremony. Because the Lord's Supper is a time for remembering Jesus and praising God, we do not want to be distracted by much eating. It may be that this is the reason why the efforts to recombine the Lord's Supper and a regular meal turn out to be so clumsy and unsatisfying. The food confuses the ceremonial side of our gathering just as the ceremony would inhibit the enjoyment of a meal.

The meal, now stylized and formalized, takes the emotions generated by biological life and transfers them to the interactions of groups of people. When we eat, we feel happy, relaxed, confident; and when eating becomes a ritual these same feelings become attached to our group associations. Happiness becomes joy, relaxation becomes peace, confidence becomes trust. All is based on the salvation which God achieves in Jesus Christ and is experienced in company with others similarly blessed. Thus the natural delights of eating are transferred to our group associations which become infused with these qualities.

This relatively simple transfer of emotion is complicated by the nature of the ingredients of the meal. In the Lord's Supper we eat bread and drink wine, but from the church's earliest years these simple foods are perceived through the lenses of Jesus' own words. While holding bread, he said "my body given for you," and while holding the cup, he said "my blood shed for you."

The transfer of emotional power is thus intensified. Blood is the sign of life itself and any meal that calls attention to blood evokes a very strong emotion of personal involvement. Thus the Lord's Supper is an especially intense example of the mealtime transfer of personal feelings to the activity and meanings of groups. What does the shedding of blood signify? Pain and sacrifice, courage and honor, love and devotion. These qualities of life are transmitted to the community that gathers in the name of Christ when they eat and drink bread and wine, flesh and blood.

This dual foundation for meal imagery has contributed to a long-term ambivalence in the emotional character of the Lord's Supper. Sometimes the delight of natural feasts has been stronger, sometimes the dreadful fascination that is associated with all of life's bloody experiences. Even in New Testament times this contrast was present. Joyful exuberance may have been the earliest quality. Christians met together "with glad and generous hearts" (Acts 2:46), excited because Jesus had risen from the dead. He joined them in their meals, making their joy even greater. With this beginning, the unrestrained festivity described in 1 Corinthians 11 is understandable. The party was getting out of hand. What the early church was forgetting, Paul brought back to mind with his sober emphasis upon Christ's suffering. His theology of the cross tempered the church's excessive merriment at communion.

Yet from that time the two strains continued: the Lord's Supper as joyful feast of the saved, the foretaste of "the lamb's bridal feast in heaven," (Revelation 19:6-10) and the Lord's Supper as remembrance of his passion and participation in his death. Roman Catholic and Protestant Christians have leaned toward the somber side of the tradition. Some of us sing hymns about the cross while others talk about the sacrament of the body and blood of Christ. The prevailing quality of the typical service is somber and sober, as befits an event based on something so dreadful as the official torture and execution of an innocent man.

Because this sober side of communion is dominant in our experience, it may be a surprise for the service to be called a feast of *joy.* I have already indicated how it can be called a feast even though the eating is only ceremonial. It is now time to discuss the meaning of the joy that is expressed in the Lord's Supper. Its joy is contemplative or meditative. Rather than being an emotion generated by an experience right then, an experience that is fun in itself, the joy of the Lord's Supper is the remembrance of significant events and the resulting ideas that are appropriate to such a memory.

An anniversary dinner is contemplative joy. It may also be immediate delight, generated by the good food, pleasant conversation, and momentary freedom from the normal duties of the evening. Even more, however, the anniversary focuses the previous years of marriage, the fading memories of courtship, the color of the wedding, the first night together, the mystery of childbirth and child rearing, the struggle and excitement of the years that two people have shared with each other. Although the man and woman may not mention all of these in their conversation, their evening out elicits the bond of love and good will that makes their life together good. This contemplative or meditative joy is restrained and calm, yet rich and inexpressibly wonderful to experience.

Contemplative joy takes place when a family gathers for dinner after laying a loved one to rest. The death rites are completed, public tears have been wept, the major ceremonies have been done decently, perhaps even with a flourish. And now they gather—spouse, children, brothers and sisters, life long friends—for food, maybe carried in by the church, maybe fixed by a family member. The funeral is recounted and the minister's work appraised, anecdotes about the deceased recalled, grudges half-confessed. The evening bears the marks of the sorrowful occasion that has brought it about. Yet an underlying glint of brighter hue shows through. Life is affirmed to be good. The dead person's positive qualities are selectively remembered. The ambiguities of the family's corporate life are transcended by the mysterious experience of acceptance of that life and of one another who share it. Again, the experience is an austere, intellectual, and real kind of joy.

Religious ritual is similarly contemplative joy. This quality is especially evident in the Old Testament psalms which intersperse laments and acclamations of joy. Psalm 31, for example, cries out:

"I will rejoice and be glad for thy steadfast love, . . . "
Yet it also pleads for help:

"Be gracious to me, O Lord, for I am in distress;
my eye is wasted from grief,
my soul and my body also."
When life is so hard, with so little cause of happiness, how can there be joy? It can be present if joy is contemplative rather than

spontaneous, the product of reflection upon God's goodness rather than the result of some momentary experience of pleasure. Religious joy is based upon a vision of life that is believed to be good whatever the outward circumstances. Persisting through all kinds of discouraging experiences, it comes as comfort when people are discouraged and challenge when they are complacent.

One of the functions of religious ceremonies is to keep alive this contemplative joy, by reminding people of the reasons for rejoicing and encouraging them to do so. The Lord's Supper does this very thing. It is conducted on stated occasions rather than when people feel like it. The words and actions refer specifically to the sources of our faith—to God the loving creator, to Jesus who laid down his life for us, to the ever present Spirit who gives us power and peace for life. Even in its most austere forms, the Lord's Supper affirms that life is good, that there is hope in the midst of tragedy and power in the face of tribulation. Joy as an idea, as an enduring state of mind, is summoned up so that people who might not in any way feel cheerful can at the same time experience joy. Having developed this inner sense, they are then able to live their daily life more effectively, and to rise above temptation, pain, sluggishness of spirit, fear, and confusion.

What I have done is claim that the Lord's Supper is a feast of joy in a very special sense. Feast means a highly stylized, ceremonial meal; and its joy, rather than being an immediate experience of personal delight, is instead an idea of what life can be and is in Jesus Christ. This religious ritual is genuine. Despite its ceremonial and intellectual character, it is a major contributor to significance in life because it shapes the inner experience of persons.

The way we think about things has much to do with what happens to us. Persons who are afraid of life meet ghosts in every possible place, whereas those who are confident about themselves tend to be met in life by positive and supporting experiences. People who believe that life is good and to be received with gratitude are able to rise above distressing and discouraging conditions. Their prevailing attitude counts for much and religious ceremonies such as the Lord's Supper create and sustain such attitudes. This symbolic meal, that presents a contemplative form of joy, is the source of power for life.

21

From Natural to Spiritual

This symbolic feast expressing contemplative joy is the carrier of meanings that are important to Christians. Two religious values expressed in this act of worship are extensions of the normal functions of meals: *nourishment* and *companionship*. Both the devotional and the theological meanings that the church attaches to the Lord's Supper come from these elemental aspects of eating a meal.

Nourishment is natural and normal. All people must eat and drink if they are to stay alive, to grow and develop, and to maintain the ordinary tasks of life. Although it is possible to supply nutriments in artificial ways such as intravenous feeding, eating and drinking are the ways that most of us receive life needs. We'd rather live by pancakes and leafy green vegetables than by IV's. The Lord's Supper is often called the sacrament of growth or maturation. If it is in baptism that new Christians are born, then it is in the Lord's Supper that they receive the nourishment they need for the sustaining of life. While baptism occurs once in a person's life, the Lord's Supper comes repeatedly and often.

But what is the content of this spiritual meal? Obviously, not protein and calories. Jesus' own words state it (Mark 14:22, 24): "Take, this is my body. . . . This is my blood of the covenant, which is poured out for many." Again, the word blood comes into the discussion. In the first chapter I pointed out one of its meanings when used in Christian worship: it is a ritual symbol that transfers powerful emotions from basic life experiences and applies them to values held by communities. In this chapter, flesh and blood are used differently, as the very ingredients of the religious meal that we eat. "He who eats my flesh and drinks my blood abides in me, and I in him" (John 6:56). What does Jesus mean by this statement? How does the Lord's Supper nourish us for the Christian life?

A few of the people who followed Jesus were wealthy, well-placed persons like Zacchaeus, Nicodemus, and the rich young ruler. Yet even they were made frantic by their experiences of futility. Think how much deeper was the despair of the crowds who were fully exposed to life's pain without the insulation provided by wealth and privilege. No wonder they crowded around Jesus who was himself so poor that he didn't even have his own place to rest at night, but had to sleep outside or accept the hospitality of friends; who spoke words that lighted fires in their own hearts even while those same words silenced their oppressors; who touched people and made them well; who by praying over bread and fish could feed a multitude. We who can remember presidential campaigns that promised jobs for all who want them, and who right now are crying out because of the high cost of food, can understand why those crowds long ago tried to seize Jesus and make him king.

The event described in John 6, during which he called himself the bread of life, was a crisis for Jesus. He had come on a mission to give life, not on a campaign to be elected king. What he now had to do was help the people understand his mission and invite them to accept the gift of life he could give. So the day after he fed the multitude, he told them the real meaning of his actions. The bread he had to give them was not food for the table nor bribes for their votes. Rather the bread which he had come to

23

hand out was of an entirely different order.

"As the living Father sent me, and I live because of the Father, so he who eats me will live because of me" (John 6:57).

These words were so blunt that in early days Christians were sometimes accused of cannibalism. In this same chapter Jesus gives two explanations of what he means.

The first of them appears in John 6:35-50 where Jesus uses the terms metaphorically.

"I am the bread of life; he who comes to me will never hunger, and he who believes in me will never thirst" (John 6:35).

To eat the bread of life is here a dramatic way of saying to believe in Jesus as Son of God and Savior. This metaphor makes sense. Without food and drink the body withers and dies. Without something to believe in, something to hold to when life is threatened, something to pull one forward toward goals and dreams, life is flat and soon becomes unbearable. A compelling faith is bread and drink to every person. And Jesus says to us: Believe in me, and in the one who sent me, and you will truly live. As one young man put it, after spending a year in one especially vibrant church: "During this year I have moved out of bare existence into living." That is what Jesus means when he invites us to eat his flesh and drink his blood. "I am the bread of life; he who comes to me will never hunger, and he who believes in me will never thirst."

Beginning in verse 51 there is a second explanation of Jesus' "I am the bread of life" saying. In this second explanation eating and believing are no longer presented as two ways of saying the same thing. Rather, Jesus asks people literally to eat his flesh and drink his blood. How could this be? The question is ours, not theirs. Nowhere in the New Testament is it discussed. Rather, there is an implicit understanding that when they ate the bread and drank the wine, Jesus gave them his very life as their food.

When John wrote his gospel, Christians had already been meeting together for a long time. For half a century or more, they had assembled at least once each week to "break bread together." They followed Jesus' own example and said the very words they remembered him to have said at the last supper he ate with the disciples before his death. At first there were few philosophers or intellectuals, few people to raise questions about the meaning of the words being used. They were common people who had felt themselves dead and now had come to life again. And it was all because of Jesus who had given his body and blood for them. At the Lord's Table they didn't ask questions; they found purpose, hope, meaning, power, courage, all coming from Jesus who had

said: "For my flesh is food indeed, and my blood is drink indeed.
. . . He who eats this bread will live forever" (John 6:55, 58b).

They knew also that this eternal life of which Jesus spoke had
already begun, right here in this world of pain and hard work,
loneliness, disappointment, old age, injustice. Experiencing this
new life at the Lord's Table, the disciples remembered again
Jesus' feeding of the multitude and his efforts the next day to explain. And this latter part of John 6 contains that remembrance,
its truth ratified by their living experience, its meaning un-
questioned by these people who knew that Christ living in them.

In his commentary on John's gospel, Raymond Brown calls
attention to the parallel between this chapter and the regular
Sunday service of preaching and the Lord's Supper. Jesus' first
explanation emphasizes faith, which comes to us when we hear
his teachings. In the first part of the service, the church reads
the Bible that tells about him and it preaches the message
of eternal life that he promises. Jesus' second explanation
emphasizes his self-sacrifice that has released life-giving power
into this troubled world. In the second part of the service
Christians stand again at the foot of the cross when they break
bread, his body, and drink from the cup, his shed blood. Every
Sunday the church recreates, through the power of Word and
Holy Spirit, the dynamics of Jesus' encounter with the crowd. He
becomes food for Christians when they believe in him. He
becomes their food when they participate, through the bread and
wine, in his sacrifice on the cross.

In later generations some Christians have focused strongly
upon the literal meaning of flesh and blood. Their personal
religious experience and their systematic ways of describing it
have both been anchored to the belief that when Jesus said this
is my body he meant exactly that. Of course, the bread has continued to appear to be bread and the wine to be wine. Yet
through these external appearances a greater reality has been
perceived—the very life of Jesus, his life in its most real and
effective form.

This emphasis on the literal meanings is expressed in the
hymn "Bread of Heaven":

Bread of heaven, on thee we feed,
For thy Flesh is meat indeed;
Ever may our souls be fed
With this true and living Bread;
Day by day with strength supplied,
Through the life of him who died.

Vine of heaven, thy Blood supplies
This blest cup of sacrifice;
Lord, thy wounds our healing give,
To thy cross we look and live:
Jesus, may we ever be
Grafted, rooted, built in thee.

What the tongue and eye cannot discern, the heart and mind can. In some churches this understanding of the Lord's Supper has led to a deep sense of awe, expressed by paying close attention to the elements on the table, protecting them from careless use or handling, and once communion is over disposing of the remaining bread and wine reverently, lest Christ himself be desecrated.

Other Christians, while willing to use the language of nourishment in their prayers and theologies, have more often used words taken from the second natural function of eating, which is companionship. In a sense, companionship is itself a spiritualization of the basic act of eating, since we can eat and drink alone, and often do. Yet human beings, in contrast to animals, express their gregariousness by sharing meals. Those who live alone are often subject to nutritional problems because they don't fix the right things to eat and sometimes those things they do eat and drink are inadequately digested. Most of us have come to the place in our social development that only when mealtime is shared is its full value released. So closely tied are eating and companionship that we tend to create small, symbolic meals in order to encourage conversation and communication. We have a cup of coffee together in order to talk with each other; and we serve tea and cookies when we get together to honor a visitor.

The Lord's Supper is the occasion for companionship—with God and with each other. Long before the Christian era Jewish people used special meals this way. In fact, communion with God seems to have been one of the major values of Old Testament sacrifices. They provided a way for Israel to pour out its soul to God and to receive his response. The reference to divine companionship through the Lord's Supper is implied in Paul's discussion of food offered to idols (1 Corinthians 10:14-22). By eating food sacrificed to idols, he says, people become partners with them; and in similar fashion he infers that when people partake of food at the Lord's Table they enjoy communion with God.

This companionship with the divine is a special instance of what all of life is intended to be—the basis for fellowship with God. The natural world was itself the place where God and people met. Adam and Eve conversed with God in the garden, in the cool of the day, until their sin caused the corrupting of this friendship. Then the world became a curse, the cause of hard work, pain, and suffering. Thus the special meals, sacrifice in the Old Testament and the Lord's Supper in the New, provided a way whereby a portion of that companionship could be recovered. These meals were signs of what all of life in this world was intended to be and could become.

In the New Testament this aspect of companionship with God was obscured by the fact that the more immediate reference of the Lord's Supper was companionship with Jesus. He had told them to break bread in order to remember him; and in the early days that remembrance was so vivid that they could affirm that they met him at the table. For example, two followers of Jesus walking to Emmaus were joined by a stranger. When he broke the bread at the evening meal, they recognized that he was Jesus (Luke 24:13-35). Yet as Jesus said to Philip, "He who has seen me has seen the father" (John 14:9). Although it took a long time for the church to straighten out its doctrine of Jesus and his relation to God, these Christians early were convinced that there was a fundamental identity of what appeared to be two divine beings.

This sense of companionship with God, experienced through Jesus of Nazareth, has found its way into hymns. One example comes from the Eastern Orthodox Tradition and is marked by a profound sense of awe:

Let all mortal flesh keep silence,
And with fear and trembling stand;
Ponder nothing earthly minded,
For with blessing in his hand,
Christ our God to earth descendeth,
Our full homage to demand.

From the Lutheran tradition comes this hymn:

Deck thyself, my soul, with gladness,
Leave the gloomy haunts of sadness,
Come into the daylight's splendor,
There with joy thy praises render
Unto him whose grace unbounded
Hath this wondrous banquet founded;
High o'er all the heavens he reigneth,
Yet to dwell with thee he deigneth.

In both of these hymns the Lord's Supper is presented as the occasion when Christians encounter Jesus who is himself the manifestation of God. This is companionship that is indeed powerful.

What about today? How can this kind of meaning still be experienced in the Lord's Supper? Perhaps it happens in isolated instances: when an astronaut partook of bread and wine during an early flight around the moon, when this simple meal is shared during a religious retreat, when a man and woman are pledging each to the other in marriage. At such times the communicative possibilities reach their fullest potential and human hearts become aware of this companionship with God. On ordinary Sundays it happens too, when those who share the meal are open to the possibility. The regular Sunday service is much like a family meal. Frequently, the conversation is minimal, scarcely more than the minimum needed for civility, while at other times the exchange of experience, idea, and conviction sparkles with light and verve. While with a family the occasion or circumstances have some influence on the discussion, the attitude of the persons is even more important. Each time they come to the table they bring a readiness to enter into the companionship, a readiness that is met or repulsed by the others who share the meal with them.

God the divine companion is always ready to enter fully into companionship, yet his readiness is only partially reciprocated by those who come to the table. Yet there are some Sundays when a combination of factors—recent experiences, mental alertness, physical condition—make an entrance into full companionship possible. What is always potential does take place.

The table companionship is not only with God, but with the other persons who gather together around the loaf and cup. There we have fellowship with other Christians. That human companionship is with Christians of all times and places. "For I received from the Lord what I also delivered to you" (1 Corinthians 11:23).With these words Paul begins his reciting of the words of institution at the Lord's Table.

When they do this same thing, Christians everywhere are joining Paul at the table, and not only Paul but Stephen the first Christian martyr, and John on the Isle of Patmos. We are united with Augustine and St. Francis, Luther and Calvin, Jonathan Edwards and Henry Ward Beecher, all of whom regularly stood at the Lord's Table reciting these words. Gathered in the congregation are the faithful of all the ages: Mary the mother of Jesus, the jailor in Philippi, Constantine and Charlemagne, St. Teresa, Christians in Plymouth Plantation, and the faithful people who brought the gospel westward.

There are times when I personally feel the ties with people of former times. Standing on the site of the Marcus and Narcissa Whitman memorial near Walla Walla, Washington, looking at the century-old wagon tracks coming around the hillside, I felt my kinship with those pioneer missionaries. My first Sunday in Somerset, Indiana, with the sounds and smells of late summer bombarding my senses, I became aware of the men and women who had built that little brick church, there been married, and from that place buried. When I hold the silver chalice, given to the seminary by the Christian Church in Edwardsport, Indiana, I can hear elders through the years repeating Paul's words. I drink from the same cup as did a great many Christians whose names I'll never know.

Although this companionship is a thing of the spirit more than of the flesh, it is true and it is real. The enduring objects of this material world do link people together in a companionship of mind that affects our actions. After walking through the house where he lived, touching the bed in which he died, walking over his grave, and standing in his octagonal study, I knew a kinship with Alexander Campbell that reading his books had never conveyed. His writings connected me to his thought, whereas the physical artifacts connected me to his life as a breathing human being.

Connection to "a people" is one of our most basic human needs. We cannot endure when cut adrift from our place in historical continuity. We have to know that we belong. The Lord's Supper helps establish this connection without which life would be very difficult to bear.

At the Lord's Table we are established as companions of the other people of the congregation where we gather. Every place consists of several groupings of people which, despite overlapping each other, are separate and distinct. Each group organizes its life around specific functions or purposes, and it has ways of connecting its people together. A service club performs community services and gathers its members together for meals, business, and programs. A trade organization promotes the business of its members and enforces guidelines for common action. And a church seeks to relate persons to God through Jesus Christ. A major factor in the achieving of this purpose is the regular gathering of these people around potent signs of God's reality, presence and power. Of these signs, the Lord's Supper is probably the most important. Sharing in that meal, we are united with others from the community who also are responding to God's call in Christ: to a young mother trying to quiet her restless child, to an aged widower scarcely able to sustain the

29

burden of life longer, to people caught up in the pressures of making a living and distributing it equitably to the generations dependent upon them. They all come together around the Lord's Table and for a little while are bound up into the church which seeks to follow Jesus.

This aspect of companionship is authentic even on those occasions when we come to church and speak to no one except in the patterned language of the service. When travelling, one might visit Saturday evening mass in a strange city and congregation. After the service, it is quite possible that no one greets the stranger, yet a form of community still is present. Out of all the people in this city, these few believe in Jesus and are eager to follow him. On such occasions one may feel no need to engage in conversation, yet, be heartened by knowing that these people are there; and afterwards, when seeing some of them in a restaurant eating supper, one will know that he is with friends.

Human companionship at the Lord's Table may include the chance to communicate directly with others who also are there. When we come together in church, it usually is in the same place with the same people, week after week. We cannot help but learn their names, discover their ideas, develop a sense of kinship with them. For some people this contact will always be superficial, never reaching the intensity that could be called companionship. For a great many people, however, interaction in church is so strong that the relationships there formed are among the most important in life. This is true despite the fact that the Lord's Supper does not permit informal and sustained conversation as does an ordinary family meal. In fact, the communion service is so tightly knit, so highly patterned, that nearly all words and actions are prescribed, leaving little place for the ordinary exchange of ideas and of life.

While I do not want to defend stilted and ineffective forms of common life, I do want to affirm that the Lord's Supper in its full context does provide exchange. Before we take our seats we talk with each other; and afterwards too. In some congregations the service provides opportunity for sharing concerns, expressing joys, and discussing needs. In all of these ways our companionship is established upon what has brought us together, faith in Christ, a faith which we express in the actions at the table of the Lord.

Despite the fact that the feast of joy is the bond of our unity in Christ, it often has been a cause of division, as I realized anew one January morning when I was one of eighteen persons assembled in St. James Chapel in the Cathedral of St. John the

30

Divine, New York City. Several of the group were catholic and the rest of us were protestants of a wide variety of types and beliefs. We shared in the celebration of the Lord's Supper according to the order developed and published by the Consultation on Church Union. When the bread and wine were distributed, twelve persons ate and drank while six did not. Four persons in the list of conference delegates had not attended, of whom two would have taken communion and one refused, while the fourth deliberately stayed away as a sign of the urgency of the question and his distress over it.

How strange it is that Christians cannot sit down together at the church's family meal. When do we more need to be strengthened by Christ and supported by one another than when meeting as strangers in a modern city—the center of poverty and unconscionable wealth, blight and unexpected loveliness, of loneliness, despair, and pain? At such a time we few Christians in an alien world need to be nourished and refreshed. Yet the sacrament given for that very purpose divides us even further. Although we can read the Bible and pray together, we cannot share in the feast of joy.

The use of the Lord's Supper as an instrument of division began in the New Testament itself. The church in Corinth had made the feast of joy into an act of drunkenness, gluttony, and uncharitable conduct so terrible that Paul accused them of "profaning the body and blood of the Lord" and of eating and drinking judgment upon themselves (1 Corinthians 11:27-29). Their eating and drinking to excess was but part of the wrong they were committing. Probably more serious was the fact that the church was being divided into factions by this service. They would begin with a meal, probably carried in by the families much as happens in fellowship meals even now. Some were able to bring ample stores, while others were too poor or were unable to bring anything because they were slaves. Instead of all sharing equally in the food and drink, however, those who brought it consumed it to excess, leaving the others hungry. Paul condemned their selfishness and divisiveness. He called them back to a remembrance of the cross and the seriousness of the supper. The damage was done and the sacrament of unity was already a means of separating Christians from each other and from their savior.

There is a discouraging history of similar episodes. Whereas in Corinth the division was sociological, dividing rich from poor and slave from free, it has often been of other types. The Lord's Supper has divided people into religious classes—clergy against laity, members of religious orders against those not committed to a specialized religious life, orthodox against heretical. It has been used to draw the line that divides people into language, ethnic, or racial groups. It has been a disciplinary instrument. In order to punish sinners, people have been refused the right to the Lord's Supper. Or it has been opened only to those who show a piety of a certain intensity or theology of a certain kind.

The Lord's Supper can be used in this divisive way because it is so important to the church's life. Just as a child is sometimes punished by being sent away from the table, thus deprived not only of food but of companionship, so Christians have been disciplined by the church, separated from the table fellowship in order to be brought to repentance and new life. This pastoral function, however, has sometimes been forgotten and the separations imposed upon persons have been caused by arrogance, selfishness, insensitivity, or some other sin, on the part of the church itself or of its leaders. Those who control the sacrament thus are using it for their own personal purposes. They may not recognize what they are doing. Their actions may be motivated by good intentions, but the division comes anyway.

Whatever the initial cause of the separation, whether it be the preservation of the church's integrity or the result of human pride, the division often is made permanent in custom, church law, and theology. Consequently, generation after generation of Christians are made strangers to each other because of the debate between two monks in the ninth century, Luther and Zwingli in the sixteenth, Methodists and Anglicans in the eighteenth, or two feuding groups in the twentieth.

These centuries of division are losing their power over us, and we are beginning to experience once again the fellowship which the Lord's Table is to express. We are dealing seriously with the religious fact that at the moment of communion we are truly united with our savior and with each other however separated we seem to be in our public and institutional life.

Our experience of the Lord's Supper can be compared to the rings on a target. At the center, the bull's eye, is the actual experience of celebrating the Lord's Supper. Here, despite the wide variety of ceremony and language, there is a remarkable similarity of experience. Christians of all times and places do receive at the table the divine food they need and experience the companionship they crave.

Around this central experience there develops a collection of prayers, hymns, and devotional materials which are used to describe what happens to us when we participate in the feast of joy. Here, too, there is widespread unity. In the hymnal now used by my church, communion hymns come from several periods in the church's life, starting with the second century. They were written by Christians from eight or nine traditions, including Roman Catholic, Moravian, and Lutheran. Here too there is a clear demonstration of unity at the Lord's Table that is greater than our separations.

It is the outer ring that reveals our separations, the group of technical explanations and official church policies that define the Lord's Supper and protect it from abuse. Here we are sharply divided from one another. Botanists agree so long as they *enjoy* the wild flowers of the Rocky Mountains—the sticky geranium, scarlet gilia, American bistort, and phacelia. They can even agree most of the time in their descriptions of color, leaf structure, and plant habits. Where they begin to differ from each other is in the more technical business of analysis and classification. Which flowers are related to which, and how? How many species are there? And so on. The botanical classifications help us organize our experience of wild flowers (after all there are some 5,000 varieties in the Rocky Mountains alone), to remember those experiences, and to explain them to others. Classifying flowers gives jobs to botanists, provides the occasion for their writing books, and makes it possible for people like me to buy them and be helped in my efforts to intensify my experiences of wild flowers in the mountains. Yet the charts and books are always secondary, always subject to correction, whereas the direct experience of seeing, touching, and smelling a flower near the summit of Togwotee Pass in Wyoming is always primary and always true.

Theologians and church lawyers do work that is important. They help us organize our experience, evaluate it, remember and preserve it, pass it on to the next generation. Yet their work is always to be subject to the basic experience, which is the direct participation in the Lord's Supper. Here we are in touch with the fact of religious life. And here Christians are united with Christ and each other regardless of how they may differ in their theologies and regulations.

A Family Meal

To this point I have assumed that the Lord's Supper is a permanent feature in the life of the church. While I have referred to its origins in the religious life of the Jewish people, my major interest in these first chapters has been to explore the meaning of this religious meal. I now want to talk about this assumption of permanence by showing how the feast of joy came to be so important in the church's life and explaining why this way of worshipping remains so firmly fixed.

Every year my mother used to can an amazing amount of green tomato mince meat (tomatoes, apples, and raisins but no meat) and candied prune conserve. She also baked bread regularly, and did all of this with a wood burning stove. My boyhood memories are filled with parker house rolls and conserve, of enough mince pie for two pieces each for father and sons. It is hard to think of Thanksgiving at my mother's house without those wonderful foods. For a good many years I have lived with a different cook and our menu is different. It has its own main features and the family knows what to look forward to for Christmas dinner and the procession of meals that follow.

Family traditions are not bound by law, yet they are firmly fixed. They grow up through a combination of practical needs (after all, something has to be done with green tomatoes after the frost, and they are cheap), happy experiences, and the interests of cooks and consumers. Once established, these customs resist change and often pass from one generation to another. I first ate checkerboard cake, one of my wife's specialties, at my mother-in-law's house, and she gave us the pans my wife uses. While these customs contribute much to the texture of family life, they also restrict it. Why not leg of lamb at Thanksgiving instead of turkey? Or chocolate eclairs at Christmas instead of fruitcake? I like both substitutes, yet the character of the dinners somehow would not be right if the established customs were set aside and something new put in their place.

Organizations are very much like families in that customs arise, gradually becoming so intertwined with the corporate identity that it is almost impossible to change or drop them. American customs include such odd elements as Easter eggs in the spring, fire works on the Fourth of July, and jack-o'lanterns in October. Although we do not have to have any of these things, they continue to be present and many of us find them included in our memories of life here. Schools have their traditions, as do lodges and unions, service clubs and scouting organizations.

The church is a special kind of community whose life also is made up of customs that add color, meaning, and continuity to all who participate in its fellowship. The uniqueness of the church is that it is made up of persons whose experience of salvation comes from Jesus of Nazareth. Its customs provide a way for each new generation to experience that salvation and to be kept in it.

The importance of salvation is clear in the New Testament. On Pentecost, Peter's sermon resulted in an outcry from his hearers: "What shall we do?" Peter told them: "Repent and be baptized everyone of you in the name of Jesus Christ for the forgiveness of your sins; and you shall receive the gift of the Holy Spirit." Later he exhorted them: "Save yourselves from this crooked generation." They were baptized and immediately became jubilant members of a new community of faith (Acts 2:37-47). This theme of salvation, made explicit in the sermons of the New Testament, is implicit in other writings. Paul's statements in the book of Romans are especially eloquent. One remarkable passage is the eighth chapter which concludes by reciting how safe we are when we are united to Christ. Twice he lists enemies rendered ineffective by divine love. The first list is impressive enough: tribulation, distress, persecution, famine, nakedness, peril, and sword (Romans 8:35). Then comes the second list in which Paul seems to throw all caution to the wind: death, life, angels, principalities, things present, things to come, powers, height, depth, and anything else in all creation. None of these, says Paul, "will be able to separate us from the love of God in Christ Jesus our Lord."

This salvation is marked by trust in God and love for people around us. Throughout the Bible God is described as our divine parent. Sometimes the imagery is maternal, as in Isaiah 66:12-14, where God speaks to the Hebrews:

"As one whom his mother comforts,
    so I will comfort you."

More often the imagery is drawn from the analogy of fatherhood, as in Romans 8. In either case, the emphasis is upon God's character and actions, upon divine love, mercy, faithfulness, and high hopes for the human race. The God made known to us by Jesus of Nazareth is strong and magnificent, yet sensitive and sympathetic to our condition. Such a one inspires trust and peace.

This God also inspires us to a particular relationship to the people around us, to treat them as God treats us. We who are loved are to love, we who are forgiven are to forgive, we who are challenged to begin again are to encourage others to undertake a new life. The salvation which Jesus gives pushes us forward toward God and outward toward those around us.

This church family comes together regularly in activities that are motivated by this experience of salvation. Christians assemble to carry on the public honor of God and to show the world what God is like. The biblical canticle based on Psalm 95 states the first intention well:

Come, let us sing to the Lord;
    let us shout for joy to the Rock of our salvation.
Let us come before his presence with thanksgiving
    and raise a loud shout to him with psalms.

For the Lord is a great God,
    and a great King above all gods.

In his hand are the caverns of the earth,
    and the heights of the hills are his also.
The sea is his, for he made it,
    and his hands have molded the dry land.

Come, let us bow down and bend the knee,
    and kneel before the Lord our Maker.
For he is our God,
and we are the people of his pasture and the sheep of his hand.
    Oh, that today you would hearken to his voice!

In Genesis it says that God created human beings in his own image. They were to be his standard bearers in the world, to declare to all that they belong to God and to show others what God expects of them. The church continues that tradition. Christians work to make God known to the world. They try to obey him and they call upon others to do so too. In their public meetings they acclaim the fruits of the Christian life, such qualities as love, joy, and self-sacrifice, and try to practice those qualities. They invite others to these meetings in the hope that they too will come to know God and to live that new life that he gives.

If we praise God and testify to his love when we come together, does it matter how we do those things, what words we use, what rituals, what ceremonies? Pure logic might answer by saying that any words or actions that lead to these results are to be encouraged. Family life, however, is rarely controlled by that kind of logic. Instead, as my earlier comments about green tomato mince meat and jack-o'lanterns were meant to show, a family's life is shaped by the accumulation of past experiences. As the family of God, the church not only is bound by the desire to praise and testify. It also is determined to accomplish these tasks in specific ways which grew out of its early experiences when the Apostles were leading its life. It now is time to describe the beginnings of Christian worship more fully than was done in the earlier chapters.

One set of customs was carried over from generations of religious life centered in Jewish synagogues. In every community the faithful would gather to read from the law and the prophets and listen to preaching, to sing the psalms and to pray. Although each synagogue had its own way of doing these things, the basic order of the service was the same across the world. Even the wording of the major prayers was close to being identical—in Jerusalem and Jericho, Antioch and Alexandria. Jesus attended the synagogue, and even after the church was established

Christians continued that practice for a time. Early in the church's life, however, Christians found that their belief in Jesus made them so different from their countrymen that they had to move out and make their own assemblies. Yet, the custom of reading scripture and preaching, singing psalms, and blessing God in prayers continued with them.

This family tradition has now endured for 2,500 years, and customs that old are likely to stay with us. Sometimes people try to set aside Bible reading in favor of some other kind of public reading in worship. Or they decide that the psalms are too archaic for modern tastes. Yet the Bible and the psalter continue to be staples in our church family's public life.

Equally important in the church's customary life is the feast of joy. When we look back on the beginnings of the Christian family, we can see how natural it was that this custom develop. The Gospels and Acts frequently report on meals eaten by Jesus, his disciples, and by gatherings of Christians in the years following his death and resurrection. Jesus attended the wedding feast at Cana in Galilee. He was a dinner guest at the home of friends like Mary and Martha, and at the parties of prominent leaders of his community. When large crowds gathered to hear him, Jesus sometimes helped to secure food for them, and then used the event as an object lesson for some of his most important teachings. We have very little information about his daily activities during his ministry, but it is easy to imagine a large number of meals around camp fires enjoyed with his disciples as they walked through the hill country of their land.

Because they were Jews, Jesus and his disciples inherited a tradition in which meals were the central act of religious celebration. The sacrifices, celebrated at open altars from earliest times, and in the temple in later history, were meals shared with God and with each other. Annually Jews gathered in their homes for the most sacred act of the year, the Feast of the Passover. The ceremonies included joyful festivity and high religious ceremony, the purpose of which was to unite the new generation with the nation's past experience. What they remembered was the deliverance from slavery in Egypt and the recovery of their ancestral homeland. In the Passover, and in other religious meals eaten by devout Jews, they also looked forward to that time when God would give them a new deliverance, driving out the Romans and giving Jews freedom in their own land.

On the night before his death Jesus ate a meal with his closest disciples. It was the Passover season and all of the traditional meanings of hope and joy were present. Jesus used the occasion to tell his friends more about himself and his mission than he had been able to say previously. Knowing that they would continue to gather this way after he had been taken away from them, he asked them to use those meals as a way of remembering him. Although they did not then understand what he meant, they later realized it more fully. After his resurrection he appeared to them briefly on several occasions on some of which they were eating together.

In later years a meal was the Christians' distinctive act of worship, much as temple sacrifices had been for Jews before that time. At first, Christians ate a full meal, accompanied by special ceremonies with a loaf of bread and cup of wine. Later they discontinued the meal but carried on the bread and wine ceremonies. This change took place during a short period of time and everywhere throughout the church. It is likely that Paul took the lead in this change and that other apostles joined him in this major change in the Feast of Joy. In the same service they would read from Old Testament writings and from the manuscripts that were to become the New Testament. They would pray, sing hymns, preach. They took up contributions for the relief of famine victims.

In these gatherings the focus of attention was Jesus Christ and his atoning death, as is illustrated by two passages from Paul's first epistle to the Corinthian church. In one place he says: "The cup of blessing which we bless, is it not a participation in the blood of Christ? The bread which we break, is it not a participation in the body of Christ? Because there is one bread, we who are many are one body, for we all partake of the one bread" (1 Corinthians 10:16-17). In the next chapter Paul describes the tradition of the founding of the Lord's Supper. Again the emphasis is placed upon Christ's sacrifice. "For I received from the Lord what I also delivered to you, that the Lord Jesus on the night when he was betrayed took bread, and when he had given thanks, he broke it, and said, 'This is my body which is broken for you. Do this in remembrance of me.' In the same way also the cup, after supper, saying, 'This cup is the new covenant in my blood. Do this, as often as you drink it, in remembrance of me.' For as often as you eat this bread and drink the cup, you proclaim the Lord's death until he comes" (1 Corinthians 11:23-26). Whatever else they did when they came together, the Christian community remembered Jesus Christ, who was:

> ". . . manifested in the flesh,
> vindicated in the Spirit,
> seen by angels,

preached among the nations,
believed on the world,
taken up in glory" (1 Timothy 3:16).

We know very little about the style of early Christian worship. They usually met in private homes, with the result that their services may have been marked by simplicity of ceremony. The style of the synagogue seems to have been quiet and simple, and this fact may have influenced the way that Christians worshiped. Yet they were also familiar with the temple ceremonies that were more elaborate. Indeed, the more exuberant style of temple worship may have inspired the final book of the Bible with its grandiose character. Isaiah's experience eight hundred years before Jesus and that of John of Revelation one hundred years after Jesus are very much alike, as can be seen by reading the passages one after the other. The prophet was in the temple at the time he received his vision. Perhaps the New Testament writer was inspired by the annual Easter services of his church.

Isaiah's Experience in the Temple (Isaiah 6:1-8) "In the year that King Uzziah died I saw the Lord sitting upon a throne, high and lifted up; and his train filled the temple. Above him stood the seraphim; each had six wings: with two he covered his face, and with two he covered his feet, and with two he flew. And one called to another and said:

'Holy, holy, holy is the Lord of hosts;
the whole earth is full of his glory.'

And the foundations of the threshholds shook at the voice of him who called, and the house was filled with smoke. And I said: 'Woe is me! For I am lost; for I am a man of unclean lips, and I dwell in the midst of a people of unclean lips; for my eyes have seen the king, the Lord of hosts!'

"Then flew one of the seraphim to me, having in his hand a burning coal which he had taken with tongs from the altar. And he touched my mouth, and said: 'Behold, this has touched your lips; your guilt is taken away, and your sin forgiven.' And I heard the voice of the Lord saying, 'Whom shall I send, and who will go for us?' Then I said, 'Here am I! Send me.' "

John's Easter Experience (Revelation 4:6-11) ". . . And round the throne, on each side of the throne, are four living creatures, full of eyes in front and behind: the first living creature like a lion, the second living creature like an ox, the third living creature with the face of a man, and the fourth living creature like a flying eagle. And the four living creatures, each of them with six wings, are full of eyes all round and within, and day and night they never cease to sing,

'Holy, holy, holy, is the Lord God Almighty,
who was and is and is to come!'

And whenever the living creatures give glory and honor and thanks to him who is seated on the throne, who lives for ever and ever, the twenty-four elders fall down before him who is seated on the throne and worship him who lives for ever and ever; they cast their crowns before the throne, singing,

'Worthy art thou, our Lord and God,
to receive glory and honor and power,
for thou didst create all things,
and by thy will they existed and were created.' "

We have no outlines of the ancient service of worship until the middle part of the second century and even then the information is scanty. We do not know what the people said and sang; but there are clues enough that many people have tried to work out tentative descriptions. We are confident that they recited psalms and read from the Old Testament writings and from the manuscripts written by Christians. They prayed. What they may have done was use several sets of Jewish prayers, especially a group regularly used in Jewish synagogues. They revised these prayers so that they would express uniquely Christian ideas. These prayers probably followed Jewish custom of calling upon God by name, reciting a list of his attributes or actions, and then offering a doxology of praise.

We do know what services were like by the beginning of the fourth century and from that time onward the evidence is abundant and consistent. The regular service of Christian worship remained much the same from that time until the protestant reformation of the sixteenth century. Reformers like Martin Luther, John Calvin, and Thomas Cranmer made many changes in the life of the church. But the changes in worship probably affected the common people more than did any other. The reformers gave a new emphasis to the people's part in the service—using the common language instead of Latin, developing congregational song, raising up the level of preaching, restoring regular sharing in both bread and wine. The doctrine of the ministry was broadened so that the church as a whole was more directly involved.

In the years since then the uniformity of worship has been modified. Yet underneath the variations is a common purpose. It is to proclaim aloud God's great glory, to encounter once again his redeeming love in Jesus Christ, and to be strengthened for our work in all the world.

Once established, family traditions resist change. Too much is at stake—memories of early years together, the feeling of belonging to a unique group of people, even the sense of personal identity—to let the customs be altered. Several devices are used to keep things the way they used to be: complaints when changes are made, volunteering to take over some part of the custom when someone else's enthusiasm wanes, reminiscing with pictures or without. It is the family's life that is being preserved by this conserving action.

The church, as family of God, is also determined to preserve its life, and the service of worship is one place where that conservatism shows. It changes little across the generations. We cannot do otherwise than come together around the Bible, the pulpit, and the communion table. The same informal devices that are used by natural families also operate in the church. We also have complaints when things are changed, new leaders stepping in when the old lose their interest, and processes of remembering how it used to be.

This emphasis upon the traditionalism of the family meal may give the impression that we are imprisoned by the decisions and actions of previous generations. That impression corresponds to the facts of human existence, both in natural families and in communities like the church. Everything that I am and am likely to become is determined by my birth to and rearing by parents who spoke English rather than some other language, valued its correct usage, and believed in education. The fact that they were poor throughout my boyhood has also shaped my adult years. I have been pressed out of a specific mold. Similarly the church today is molded by its traditions of scripture, sermon, and supper. However free we might be theologically to do something different when we worship, the anthropology of our past life holds us in captivity.

Yet individually and corporately we do have power to change. I handle my mother tongue in a way unique to me and have passed it on to my children in a form different from that given me by my parents. The changes in values and patterns of life are subtle and delicate, yet real. They are the result of the life spirit that animates my body.

The church too is animated by a life spirit, the Holy Spirit of God himself. It is interesting that a passage of scripture that emphasizes tradition—the one in which Paul says "For I received from the Lord what I also delivered to you . . ." (1

Corinthians 11:23)—is the preface to the most significant discussion of the Holy Spirit in the New Testament. Paul was very much alive religiously, which means that the divine life spirit was at work in him. Thus, he significantly influenced the tradition which he had received and transmitted. Every generation has similarly received a tradition and then passed it on, altering it in the process. Some people, like Paul, have been unusually animated by the Holy Spirit, thus making an especially great impact in this process of transmission. Yet all of us are involved in this same sequence of receiving the tradition, modifying it, and passing it on to the next generation in altered form. Over the course of time we change the hymns we sing, revise the way we pray, and reform the way the service is conducted. While the basic structure of proclaiming the Word and serving the feast of joy continues through the generations, the Holy Spirit lives in the church and animates its life.

Blessed Be the Tie That Binds

The powers that pull at families and organizations like the church are strong and never ceasing. In order to survive, we establish structures of relationship and continuity that reinforce our strength and help us to do what we want to do.

The human family is always under stress. Careers reach out and seize parents, pulling husband and wife apart and separating them from their children. School makes its demands and casts its spells upon younger members of the family. All are tempted by friends and recreations to move away from the family. Inside the house, TV, radio and stereo have ways of stifling conversation and isolating persons one from another. Every family has to develop its own way of coping with this condition. Perhaps it is the habit of regularly eating dinner together and refusing ever to play TV or radio at that time. It may be that sitting in the same pew in church on Sundays or establishing specific guidelines about keeping track of each other's activities are parts of the form. Every family has its structure for staying together and usually there is a strong correlation between the efficiency of the structure and the strength of the family.

The church is always subject to disintegration, too. Like every other community, we are susceptible to the ordinary but vicious sins such as arrogance, insensitivity, laziness, and vindictiveness. We hurt one another by thoughtless words and actions, fall down on the job, break promises, and make unwise decisions. Able leaders are followed by inept ones, enthusiasms wane, and programs lag. The gaps between vision and reality, goals and performance, initial zeal and later moderation cause congregations to lose heart and members to fall away.

In order to counteract these tendencies toward corruption and to present the gospel to every generation, the church has developed a three-fold structure of continuity: the structure of worship, the meaning to be stated in the communion prayer, and a publicly authorized body of leaders.

Perhaps the most important of these three elements is the structure of worship. The church insists that worship be conducted at least once a week and that specific things be done during that worship.

Sunday comes once a week whether we are ready for it or not. Sunday expects something of us. We are to set aside our other employments and go to church, for God's sake and for our own. While it is true that many people follow this form only intermittently, a larger number of Christians plan their lives so that Sunday church attendance is more a normal action than an abnormal one.

The result of this insistence is that we encounter the Word, the Supper, and each other frequently enough so that the succession is cumulative. Each service of worship builds upon the previous ones in a way that might not be possible if we were to have long intervals between our assemblies. We become familiar enough with the order of worship, the language used, and the ceremonies performed that they become extensions of ourselves, just as forks or bicycles become so integrated to us that we no longer have to think how to use them. Worship done frequently unites the heart and mind, and even the muscles of the body, into an instrument

45

that we can use to praise God and be united to other Christians.

There is, of course, the danger that those things we do habitually become mechanical and empty, or that we become careless in their use. Experienced drivers, who can drive without thinking about what they are doing, sometimes drive that very way and are likely to run into something as a result. Worship done regularly can become dull and lifeless. Yet the risk is necessary, because structure keeps us close to the source of genuine religious life. In due time there is a fresh influx of the divine life Spirit and the church comes alive again.

The meaning of Sunday becomes clear when we contrast it with the meaning of the Sabbath and show how Sunday worship first came into being. On the seventh day of creation, God rested from his labors. He pronounced everything good. From that time onward, his people kept the day as holy to the Lord and thereby continuously reaffirmed the goodness of all that God had made. Yet the created order, and especially the human race, was deeply flawed by sin. For that reason Jesus died, thus breaking down the powers of evil. In his ministry he had proclaimed the coming kingdom when all things would be made right again, and by his sacrifice he released the power that would bring that kingdom into its completed form.

It was this inauguration of the kingdom of God that early Christians celebrated on the first day, the day after the ancient Sabbath. They affirmed that God can work even in this broken world of work and death. For perhaps 300 years they worshipped on Sunday even though it was simply another work day in the Roman world. On Saturday evening (the eve of Sunday) or early Sunday morning they assembled to read, preach, pray, and break bread together. Then they went about their regular work, infusing it with the living power bestowed on them by God himself.

In addition to the commitment to weekly worship, the structural element of continuity has included the shape of the service. Worship is to consist of specific parts—proclaiming the Word of God, praying for ourselves and the whole world, and celebrating the feast of joy—and they are to be conducted in a specific order. I have already described how these actions became the mainstays of the church's life and I have said something about their meaning. Here my purpose is to show the sequence of these parts, thereby indicating how they are related to each other.

Proclaiming the Word has usually combined reading portions of the Bible with preaching that connects the ancient word and the modern world. Although the Bible is a large book with com-

46

plicated contents, it still is manageable. We can become acquainted with all of it. Furthermore, the Christian community long ago accepted it as an especially authoritative expression of God's will for us. In later generations personal study of the Bible and the public use of it in worship and theology have confirmed that relationship of Scripture to God. The church says to us that when we come together we should read from the Bible. Never mind its rootage in an ancient culture, its archaic thought forms, its oddities and puzzles. In all of its strangeness and opaqueness, it still is connected to God and therefore by reading it we move toward him.

This is not to say that we should revel in its obscurity or refuse to make it understandable. It does not even mean that all other readings are to be excluded. Rather, this insistence that we read from this book means that the Bible is more important for worship than is any other book and that we are obligated to work at understanding it. Anything else we choose to read in worship has to be looked upon as a supplement to the basic material that is to command attention.

While the Bible is rooted in the ancient world, another part of the service grows out of current experience. The prayers are contemporary, voicing the pain of life and its joy. We pray for governments and those governed, for workers of every kind and artists, for parents and children, the proud and the humble. We confess our sin, ask God's forgiveness, and recommit ourselves to him. We pray for the church, asking God to bless it in its mission to the world.

The sermon bridges these two parts of worship. Preaching is anchored to scripture and its testimony to God's work long ago. Yet the sermon is also tied to human life today in all of its particularity. Preachers explore the scripture, identify God's unique activity, and state it so that people today can understand it. At the same time, they examine contemporary experience, draw out its meaning, and subject it to the scrutiny of scripture.

Following reading, preaching, and praying, we administer the feast of joy. According to the tradition of most of Christendom, ancient and modern, the Lord's Supper is a series of actions, some carried out mainly by words and others mainly by gestures and bodily movements. Some of them, such as specific references to Jesus' death, are necessary for the theological integrity of the service, while others, such as the singing of hymns, are important to give it dramatic unity and interest.

The first of these actions can be called the *approach to the table*. It is a group of words and gestures intended to focus attention upon the feast of joy. One of my most vivid memories of communion during my boyhood was the action of elders at the beginning of the service. The communion hymn was announced and while the congregation was singing the two elders for the day removed the white linen cloth from the communion elements. This combination of devotional singing and dramatic act was a striking way to get started. Since it now is less common for communion to be covered with white cloths during the rest of the service, the current approach to the table tends to be more word than gesture. There are invitations to communion, the reading of appropriate passages of scripture, brief meditations or interpretations of the meaning of the Lord's Supper. The singing of a hymn is still common practice as leaders of the communion service make their way to the table. Whatever is done, the purpose should be the same: to shift attention to the table and to help the congregation get ready to share in this important part of our worship.

The second action, often blended in with the first, is the *setting of the table with the communion elements.* In some traditions the bread and wine are carried to the table in a procession while in others they are already on the table but now are made ready for use. There was a time when the bread and wine were brought from their homes by members of the congregation. People still living have told me how their parents were responsible for making the bread and preparing the fruit of the vine for their congregations. Clearly the Lord's Supper was their sacrifice of praise and thanksgiving; the elements themselves helped to convey this meaning. Although current customs of buying commercial supplies obscure this side of communion, the basic intent of the setting of the table remains the same: to declare by our gifts that we are presenting ourselves to God in joyful obedience to the claims of Christ upon us.

Perhaps this is one of the main reasons why the bringing of money has been added to this part of the service. Since we no longer live in a barter economy, financial gifts are a more obvious expression of our vital powers than are bread and wine. The placing of substantial money offerings on the table can therefore clarify what we mean by the gifts of bread and wine.

Although this second part of the communion service is primarily gesture, words can be used significantly. Sometimes people will be invited to share in the offering and participate in communion. It is widespread custom for the congregation's role to be expressed through ceremonies like standing to sing the Doxology while the gifts are being brought to the table. Frequently there is a brief prayer by one of the leaders dedicating these gifts to God and to his service.

The third action in the feast of joy is *prayer*. Here words come into their own as the carrier of meaning for everything else that is being done. This prayer is the most important set of words in the entire service. Their theological function is to state the purpose of our worship, to sum up the meaning of everything else that we are doing together, and to present it all to God. Their dramatic function is to focus all attention upon God's wonderful act and to unify all attention upon what God does for us. The communion prayer often contains echoes of other things that have been said in the service but brings them into the light of the Cross.

The fourth action is the dramatic gesture of *breaking the bread* which is the preparation for our eating and drinking the consecrated bread and wine. Jesus broke the bread before giving it to his disciples, and Paul speaks of the meaning of this act: ". . . The bread which we break, is it not a participation in the body of Christ?" (1 Corinthians 10:16). Another of my boyhood memories is the action of the elders following their prayers. They would step around in front of the table and break the bread. We used matzos wafers, one in each tray. The elders broke them into smaller portions and the sound of their snapping could be heard throughout our small church. Other kinds of bread are now used, some of it scarcely recognizable as bread. It still can be used ceremonially. The bread tray could be lifted up while the biblical words of institution are recited. Or a small loaf or roll can be broken and used by the leaders of the service as their communion bread.

It is also common custom to make some kind of gesture with the wine. When a common cup was used, the wine was often poured from a pitcher into the chalice which was to be used by the congregation. When individual cups are used, the tray can be touched or lifted as the words are spoken.

The next act is *eating and drinking,* the logical climax in any ceremony called a feast. In some churches people go to the table, while in others the bread and wine are distributed to them in their seats. Although the manner of distribution is primarily custom, there is also a difference in symbolic meaning. When the congregation goes to the table, the fellowship with Christ risen and glorified is made prominent. When the elements are brought to the people, fellowship with Christ in our midst is suggested.

There usually is a time of quietness during the distribution of the elements, a time used by many people for their personal meditation upon the mystery of our salvation. They can be

49

helped by the words of scripture and hymnody which have been used in the service, by quiet instrumental music, and by music sung either by the choir or congregation. However this period of time is filled, there does need to be a portion of quietness sufficiently empty of distraction that personal meditation is possible.

Just as we have to start a service, so we have to *finish* it, and this is the final action of the feast of joy. Things have to be put away and the congregation prepared for what comes next. These tasks may be accomplished by gesture only—covering the empty vessels and moving away from the table. Or they can be accomplished partially through the use of words such as brief prayers of thanksgiving, a hymn, or closing scriptural sentences. When communion comes at the close of a service, the concluding act might be the benediction or dismissal.

I have arranged these six actions in a specific sequence which has been the prevailing form of the communion service throughout Christian history. Even today the great majority of the Christian family, catholic and protestant, orders the service this way. This order is based on logic as well as on theology. Only after the table is set do we give thanks and share in the meal.

Some churches do change the sequence, perhaps breaking the bread before the prayers, or taking the offering after communion. The effect of the service as a whole may not be greatly changed by this rearrangement. All together it still is an act of thanksgiving to God, remembrance of Christ, fellowship with him and with each other. The rearrangement does imply a changed relationship of the parts to each other. When the offering of money is combined with the gifts of bread and wine, there is a blending of our lives and the service of remembrance. When the offerings of money come afterwards, or are separated from communion by the sermon, the supper and the financial gifts lose the sense of their relationship to each other.

Since most of us are used to seeing a service written out in outline form, I want to close this chapter with two outlines of the service.

A. A Brief Communion Service

Opening Sentences of Scripture
Hymn of Praise
Readings from the Bible
Communion Meditation
Communion Hymn and Preparation of the Table
The Communion Prayers

Breaking of Bread and Words of Institution
The Distribution
The Dismissal

B. *The Feast of Joy in its Regular Setting*

The Beginning
    Prelude
    Call to Worship
    Hymn of Praise
    Opening Prayer
Proclamation of the Word
    Readings from the Bible
    Hymn or Anthem
    Sermon
    Invitation to Discipleship and Hymn of Commitment
    Prayers of Intercession and Supplication
The Feast of Joy
    Communion Hymn (verse one)
    Scripture Sentences or Invitation to the Table
    Gathering the Gifts
    Hymn and Presentation of the Gifts
    The Communion Prayers
    Breaking of Bread and Words of Institution
    Choral Meditation
    The Distribution
    Communion Hymn (one verse)
The Closing
    Dismissal
    Hymn
    Postlude

Offering the Communion Prayer

In the early church the form and general content of the communion prayer were based on ancient Jewish prayers. Each congregation developed its own Christian version. Once established, however, these prayers became fixed and changed very little thereafter. The words were written down and leaders of the congregation would read them or recite them from memory. There came a time when the church's ministers were no longer permitted to develop their own prayers for communion; they had to use those approved by the whole church in its region of the world.

Very late in Christian tradition a new version of the earliest tradition arose. In some parts of European protestantism, and especially in Puritan Christianity in England and the United States, the conviction arose that prayers should be taught by the Holy Spirit instead of learned from books. This led to extempore prayer, a practice which has dominated American protestantism. The prayers of the service, including those offered at the Lord's Table, have been worded at the time of praying by the person offering the prayer.

In most of the church, however, the major prayers, and especially the communion prayer, are prescribed by church bodies, published in authorized books of worship, and made mandatory for ministers and congregations. There are at least two reasons, the less important of which is that this is the way they have always done it. The more important reason is the conviction that the major prayers of the service are crucially important in the religious transactions of worshippers and God. People in these churches are unwilling that individuals, even devout and learned ministers, get in the way. To protect these religiously significant times of worship, these church bodies ordinarily lay down two rules. First, only ordained ministers are authorized to offer these prayers; and second, they must use only the texts officially approved.

The extempore approach to public prayer will continue. One reason is custom since some of us have grown up in this tradition and do not easily change. The second reason is that extempore prayer makes possible an immediacy and directness that is difficult to attain when only fixed prayer texts are used.

There are, however, two dangers in the use of extempore prayer. The first is that the prayer becomes personal rather than being representative, and the second is that the ideas expressed are unsuited to the occasion when they are offered. These dangers are greater now than formerly because church people are more widely exposed to secular ideas than they used to be. At the same time churches have failed to maintain traditional language and ideas in their common life. These two conditions inevitably lead to a thinning out of what people hear repeatedly when they attend church. Since extempore prayer is learned by hearing others offer it, this thinning out of what is heard in church inevitably leads to the weakening of the new generation's prayers.

Even though the communion prayer is offered by individuals, they speak not on their own behalf but as representatives of the congregation. Their thoughts and words give form to the hopes and intentions of the congregation. There are several things that leaders of prayer can do in order to make their public prayers representative. They can begin their preparation well before time to offer the prayer by thinking about their own lives and those of the people of the congregation. What has been happening to us? How are we handling these experiences? How have we experienced God in these recent days? For what do we want to give thanks? Or complain about? Or ask God's help? From these reflections certain common experiences, hopes, and fears are chosen to give shape to the thanksgiving for redemption, which is the major element in the communion prayer.

Some people fill their minds with these reflections but make no prior decisions about words or form of the prayer, depending upon the inspiration of the moment for the prayer itself. Others outline a prayer, but wait for the words to be given them at the time the prayer is offered. Still others write out the words in advance and offer the prayer by reading it in the service.

Whichever of these customs is adopted, there is another way of indicating the representative character of public prayer: to use first person plural forms instead of first person singular. In private and personal worship a person says *I* thank you, *I* ask you, *I* pray; but in public worship that same person says *we* thank you, *we* ask you, *we* pray.

Still another way to express the representative character of public prayer is to steer a course between being very specific and very general. The ideas should not be so specific that they embarrass or enrage persons in the congregation. When prayers are too much like this they no longer help people approach God. Some people may not want to say those specific things to God and others may be too distraught by the words to focus upon the Divine. Yet if the language is too general or abstract, it leaves people unable to take hold and to approach the Eternal One.

Even when extempore prayer is representative, there is a second danger, that it drift away from the purpose of the Lord's Supper. In brief, the communion prayer is to stay closely tied to the actions that take place at the table—bringing gifts of bread and wine, breaking the bread, and eating and drinking together. Throughout most of the church's history, the prayer has had four main elements which, when carefully phrased, provide its theological integrity: thanksgiving, remembrance, prayer for the Holy Spirit, and dedication of life. In addition to these four main parts, there will usually be the naming of God at the beginning of the prayer and a conclusion ending in *Amen.*

Thanksgiving reaches its climax in our expressing gratitude for Jesus Christ and the salvation which he has accomplished for us.

He saves us *from* our sin and its consequences. He saves us *for* a new life of peace, power, and joy. All of this he achieved by his life and teachings, by his death upon the cross and his resurrection from the dead, and by the intercessions he makes for us now. This full salvation is the climax of God's whole work of creating and sustaining life, and is the major emphasis of the prayer.

Yet this central focus is often prefaced by thanksgiving for God's other work. Some communion prayers begin by praising God for the early leaders of the Bible who led the way for Christ. Others begin the prayer by referring to creation and providential care, and then move to thanksgiving for Jesus. Some communion prayers rejoice in the experiences of God in the church and then focus upon Jesus whose sacrifice has made it all possible. The communion prayer could begin by praising God for his gift of the natural world or for the world of human culture and creativity which he inspires.

In all of these types of the communion prayer, there are two guidelines: (1) Always the dominant theme is thanksgiving to God for the saved life he gives us. (2) The general thanksgiving with which the prayer begins is always to lead to very specific thanksgiving for Jesus Christ—for his life and ministry, for his suffering and death, for his victory over death, and for his work of saving us from our sins. In giving thanks, it is common to refer to the bread and the cup with words such as: "We give you thanks for this loaf and the privilege of gathering at this table." Although these thoughts are appropriate, they are only the beginning of what needs to be said. The main emphasis of the prayers should be Jesus and his sacrifice for us: "We give you thanks for Jesus who gave his body as a sacrifice for us." Bread is the focus of this prayer and is tied in with the meaning of the Lord's Supper; but our thanks is for something far more important than a morsel of flour and water.

Remembrance is the second part of the prayer and often blends into thanksgiving so fully that these two parts are indistinguishable. Jesus himself provides this intention—that the breaking of bread is for the recalling of him. In some churches the biblical words of institution are incorporated into the prayer itself, forming the central part of the remembrance. In others these words are omitted, but other language specifically mentions Jesus and his sacrifice. In this way the church accomplishes one function of communion, to keep alive the effect of Jesus' work. The church remembers what he did and is brought again into its power. And the church recites that saving act in its prayer to God, thus pleading with him for mercy. Often the prayer refers to the loaf and cup during this act of remembrance. The bread is identified with Jesus' body, the wine with his blood. Together they represent his saving act.

The bread and wine are also used in the third part of the prayer, the *calling upon the Holy Spirit*. The Lord's Supper does look backwards to a decisive event in history when Jesus died for the sins of the world. It happened once and for all. Yet Christians live now; and they look forward to the future. These three dimensions of time are brought together by God's Holy Spirit. This fact the prayer recognizes by invoking the Spirit, calling upon him to be present so that bread and wine might be for us the body and blood of Christ, that we might become his people, that we might be cleansed of our sin and empowered for life in the world.

Already we have moved into the fourth theme, *the rededication of life to his service*. Here the offering comes into focus. By that action Christians pledge themselves to serve God and now in the prayer they state that intention explicitly.

It has been common practice in the church for the communion prayer to be concluded by the congregation. With one voice the people of God speak to him in the prayer that Jesus taught his disciples.

The elements that have been described above are illustrated in the following prayer.

Thanksgiving	God of all times and places, it is good to give you thanks:
	    for life itself,
	    for good food to eat that our bodies may be strong, and
	    for the nourishment of mind and heart.
	You are good to us and we can only begin to proclaim our gratitude and your praise.

for Jesus	Especially do we thank you, Father, for Jesus Christ
Remembrance	who by his life and ministry, his suffering and death, his resurrection and intercessions for us, saves us from our sins.
Calling on the *Holy Spirit*	Send your Holy Spirit, we pray, upon these gifts of bread and wine, and upon us. With this heavenly food nourish us and make us better disciples of our Lord.
Rededication	When we leave this house of prayer, strengthened by the feast of joy, use us in your

kingdom. We pray through Jesus Christ our
Lord. *Amen.*
Because of your love for us, we dare to pray:
Our Father in heaven,
> hallowed be your Name,
> your kingdom come,
> your will be done,
>> on earth as in heaven.
Give us today our daily bread.
Forgive us our sins
> as we forgive those who sin against us.
Save us from the time of trial
> and deliver us from evil.
For the kingdom, the power, and the glory are
> yours now and for ever. Amen.

In most church bodies there is only one prayer offered at the
table. In such a case, it is important that the one prayer include
all of the elements which should be in such a prayer. In some
other church bodies, it has been customary for two prayers to be
offered, one focusing upon the bread and one upon the cup.
Although several ways of dividing responsibility could be
developed, they all require more organization, presence of mind,
and regulation than is likely to be observed in congregations that
practice extempore prayer. If both leaders offer a complete communion prayer, one referring to the bread and the other to the
cup, each will likely compensate for any weakness the other may
possess.

It should be evident by now that the responsibility to lead extempore prayer places great demands upon those who do it.
Their words and actions are to be the vehicle by which the congregation approaches God. To do the work well requires careful
preparation. One kind of preparation has been the topic of this
chapter, the reflection out of which the ideas and words of the
prayer will come. Another kind is mental rehearsal of the
movements of the service so that those who lead are confident in
their actions. When do they go to the table? When do they hand
out the trays? When do they make their statements and offer
their prayers? When do they sit down and stand up? The Lord's
Supper is too important for the congregation to tolerate absent-
mindedness in its leaders.

It helps, too, if leaders arrive at the church and the time of service with spirit composed, braced for the work. A clear head and
sense of readiness are as important as anything else because they

allow persons to utilize fully their knowledge and personal powers.

These ways of preparation—reflecting upon the content of the prayer, mentally rehearsing the ceremony, and getting set for the service—all are aimed at a specific Sunday when a person will be the leader at the feast of joy. They are immediate and specific. Yet when engaged in week after week, they lead to a steady, enduring capacity to lead at the Lord's Table. They provide a store of ideas and expectations that are available to leaders even when they have not been able to prepare adequately for any one service.

It is fitting that leaders prepare themselves in another way that is not directed so much to any one Sunday. It is the filling of the mind and heart with ideas and language out of which the words of prayer will come. The Bible is one book to study. Another one is the hymnal with its large collection of religious verse set to music. Many of the hymns are prayers addressed to God and can be studied for their style as well as their meaning. Note the titles given to God in the hymns, the divine attributes which are listed and praised, the confessions made, the promises renewed. By reading through the hymnal and by singing or reciting hymns aloud, leaders of worship gradually acquire a stock of phrases to use when they pray. Other religious writings can be used similarly, especially collections of prayer and poetry.

Still another kind of more general preparation is the work of developing spiritual maturity. It comes, in part, through patterns of reflection, meditation, and prayer such as those mentioned above. It also comes from Christian service outside of the Sunday ceremonial: calling on the sick and shut-in, working for the increase among persons of the love of God and neighbor. The church long ago decided that God can use the sermons and prayers of evil preachers and priests. He still can do so. Yet he desires that we be perfect as he is perfect (Matthew 5:48), that our lives conform to his will for human beings. Thus no Christian, and especially no leader of word and sacrament, can ever rest contentedly in his or her sins. We all must try to establish symmetry between our lives and his. When that happens our prayers and actions at the table are infused with the strength and beauty which come from God.

Leaders of the Service

Leaders of the Lord's Supper have gone by many names: bishop, president, elder, minister, priest, pastor. Some have been salaried leaders of the church, while others have led worship without financial support. Most of these persons have been ordained, using a ceremony of prayer and the laying on of hands. Others have been authorized to serve by simpler methods of choice and installation. Some of the leaders have taken a formal course of study in the Bible and theology, while others have possessed only the learning acquired by personal study.

There is, however, a common base to all of these variations, the office of elder described in the New Testament. Of the several passages dealing with the elder, the most helpful is Acts 20. The speaker is Paul, already en route to Rome where he is to be subjected to trial, imprisonment, and execution. On the journey he frequently is met by friends and former colleagues who reminisce about their former times of joy and pain, talk about the prospects of earthly grief and heavenly delight, and console one another in the face of the trouble awaiting them.

Especially poignant is the meeting with elders from Ephesus in which Paul gives his final testimony as a free man. He had worked in that city for nearly three years (Acts 19:8-10; 20:31), probably longer than in any other place on his missionary journeys. Some of the exciting times of his ministry had been experienced with this group of leaders. Now that they were together for what was sure to be the last time, Paul opened to them his most intimate thoughts about their work as leaders of the Christian congregation. Two qualities stand out in this passage: the importance of the elders' work as guardians of the faith, and the religious character of their leadership.

These two qualities are bound together in the figure of speech, drawn from the Old Testament, which Paul used to describe their work. The clearest statement is this: "Take heed to yourselves and to all the flock, in which the Holy Spirit has made you overseers, to care for the church of God which he obtained with the blood of his own Son" (Acts 20:28). In the ancient world and in contemporary times, in primitive places and in the American West, shepherds have been responsible for overseeing the flocks, protecting them from harm, and securing pasture. Given sufficient wilderness, wild sheep and goats can shift for themselves but domestic animals need keepers.

Early in his address to these elders Paul summarized the gospel which was the nourishment needed by the church ". . . repentence to God and . . . faith in our Lord Jesus Christ" (Acts 20:21). We could paraphrase him this way: Trust in Jesus and yield yourselves to God and you will find life that is worth living. This is the word which nourishes the church. This is the message which elders are to proclaim.

As shepherds they had a second responsibility, to protect the flock from enemies. Some of these dangerous ones would come from outside. People would preach and teach some other foundation for the Christian life than the message of the kingdom, some doctrine different from the twofold call to repentence and trust in Jesus Christ. Paul knew that false teachers would arise inside the church, too. As mature persons, well founded in the genuine gospel, the elders were to protect the church from both kinds of danger. In fact, false teaching from inside could be even more dangerous than that which came from external sources. It would have the appearance of authenticity and would come with evidence of friendship. Yet these internal ideas could also lead people away from the gospel which Paul had first proclaimed.

One cannot help but draw the conclusion that for Paul the integrity of the Christian faith was the issue. Convinced that not everything which seems plausible and which carries Christian names is genuine, he depended upon the council of mature Christians to care for the congregation—proclaiming the true faith, clarifying opinion, and pointing out strange teaching.

Although Paul was confident that he himself saw the faith clearly and accurately, he knew how hard it was for individuals to care for the church by themselves. Therefore, in the congregations which he organized, he entrusted the work of oversight and nurture to groups of persons rather than to individuals. Together they could search out the gospel and evaluate new ideas with greater certainty than could any one individual. This collegial character of guardianship of the faith is an important aspect of ancient Christian insight.

Paul used a word to describe this office that could easily be misunderstood, the word overseer or guardian. Much of his talk to the Ephesian elders was an effort to keep them from making that mistake. It is always a temptation to yield to power and to use it harshly, woodenly, or smugly. Elders were not to be that kind of guardians. They had the example of Paul himself who while ministering to them did so "with all humility and with tears and with trials" (Acts 20:19). They knew of the imprisonment and afflictions which awaited him upon his arrival in Rome. Even more, they were to be inspired by the example of Jesus who gave his life and who said that " . . . it is more blessed to give than to receive" (Acts 20:35). The tenor of this message is that elders were to accept a life of hard work, misunderstanding, sacrifice, and care.

Yet they did not need to be afraid either of failing strength or of pain. They, like him, would be supported by God and "the word of his grace" (Acts 20:32). Perhaps the elders remembered Paul's own experience (reported for us in 2 Corinthians 12:7) of a "thorn in the flesh" which he had repeatedly asked that God remove. Yet each time the answer came that God's grace was sufficient. Paul was confident that the same experience would come to the elders at Ephesus. Whatever their experience of trial and pain, they would find a strong sense of support and fulfillment so that they would know that it had been worth every bit of the hardship.

Elsewhere in the New Testament there are other passages that talk about elders. A cluster of them appears in the three short books of Timothy and Titus, which together are referred to as the pastoral epistles. They were written in the third generation of the church's life (see 2 Timothy 1:5), a time in which the church's earlier enthusiasm for the gospel had grown cool. Problems which Paul had anticipated half a century earlier, in his speech to the Ephesian elders, had developed. What was needed was strengthening and regulating of the church's life, both in its doctrine and its organization.

In the ancient world, outside of the church, the word elder was used in two ways, both of which appear in the pastoral epistles. One of them was an association of older people meeting for companionship and common activity. The other was a committee or council with governmental or organizational responsibility. In Titus 2:2 the first of these uses seems to be present, whereas in passages like 1 Timothy 5:17-20 the second use seems present. The elders formed a council (1 Timothy 4:14) and laid hands upon a man set apart by a prophet for religious service (1 Timothy 1:18 and 4:14). It seems clear that they were responsible for the life of the congregation. As in Acts 20:17 the word elder is used in the plural. These writings always refer to elders rather than to elder.

A second word appears in these same passages from the pastoral epistles—the word translated overseer, guardian, or bishop. But it always is used in the singular. That is to say, the pastoral epistles speak of bishop and elders. These writings, however, do not explain the difference between these two terms. It is clear from 1 Timothy 5:17 that some of the elders did not preside or teach. Yet some of the requirements were made of elders and the bishop alike. For example, elders and the bishop were to be blameless or above reproach, husband of one wife, temperate and not quarrelsome, and able to handle their own households (compare 1 Timothy 3:1-7, which talks about those aspiring to the office of bishop, and Titus 1:5-9, which gives qualifications for elders). As best we can tell, there were in the church of that time two kinds of leaders. Some persons, the elders, cared for the church because they were mature in the Christian faith; apparently there was always a group of them in the congregation. At the same time one person, the bishop, served as administrator with special responsibility for worship, the care of the poor, and the congregation's correspondence. At least two of these functions naturally went together. Since the contributions toward the care of the poor were usually brought as part of the service of worship, the officer who was in charge of the Lord's Supper could easily be expected to supervise the distribution of those gifts.

We do not know, either from the New Testament or from later writings, how these two approaches to organization developed. Was one of the elders appointed or elected a bishop? Did they rotate the responsibility according to some agreed upon plan? Was there a bishop from the beginning who asked the association of older men to help him when the work load grew heavy?

Instead of discussing these questions, the pastoral epistles concentrate upon the manner of life that these persons were supposed to lead. Many of the qualities were not unique to Christians. Other people in the ancient world were expected to live that way too. The two conditions which seem to have been distinct were that leaders should not be newly baptized and that they should be of good reputation among those outside of the church. By the first requirement, the church hoped to assure itself of seasoned leadership and to reduce the danger that leaders would become too self-important. By the second, they hoped to assure that the church could live peaceably with the secular authorities and be on good terms with their neighbors.

The lists of qualifications refer to the marital status of elders and the bishop, using language that is difficult to understand.

1 Timothy 3:2—"Now a bishop must be . . . husband of one wife . . ."

Titus 1:5-6—". . . and appoint elders . . . if any man is blameless, the husband of one wife . . . "

1 Timothy 5:9—"Let a widow be enrolled . . . having been the wife of one husband . . . "

It seems reasonable to assume that these passages are speaking out against unfaithfulness in the marriage relationship. But do they require that one must be married at the time one serves as elder, bishop, or widow? Do they mean that one must have been married only one time? Or do they mean that one can be married only to one person at a time? This last question is the right one. The positive teaching in these passages is that those who become leaders in the church are to be *faithful to spouse*. And that is all that they say. They do not require remarriage. Nor do they rule out marriage, divorce, and remarriage.

In the generations following the church's first decades the bishop-elder pattern of ministry developed into a more formal structure of leadership. Each bishop became responsible for the spiritual care and oversight of several congregations in the regions surrounding his own church. Although the bishop's work became partially administrative, its pastoral character remained dominant. Bishops were still thought of as pastors and they continued to preach and teach, to baptize and preside over the Lord's Supper. Each of the congregations in the district was cared for by an elder who represented the bishop's spiritual oversight of that group of Christians. Bishops and elders, by that time called priests, were theologically trained, salaried, and put into their positions with a special ceremony called ordination. Paul's practice of having several elders in a congregation was no longer followed.

In all of these passages, both in Acts and the pastoral epistles, the assumption is that elders and bishops would be men. There is no command that only men were to carry those responsibilities; nor are women prohibited. But the language, especially in Timothy and Titus, is male in gender. On the one hand, we ought not be surprised at this fact since the first Christians had grown up in a culture where men dominated women. Both in Graeco-Roman life and in Hebraic tradition, there was little public life permitted to women. The church let these pre-Christian conditions continue in its life.

On the other hand, the gospel seemed so very clear that in Christ everything was to be different. The most daring statement of this new kind of life appears in Paul's letter to the Galatian church. In the early portion of this epistle he contrasted life under the law and life in Christ. The law was a severe and confining master, but the gospel was the source of freedom. Then Paul proclaims his deep conviction: "For as many of you as were baptized into Christ have put on Christ. There is neither Jew nor Greek, there is neither slave nor free, there is neither male nor female; for you are all one in Christ Jesus" (Galatians 3:27-28). In the former time only men were accepted into full membership in the religious community. Now, says Paul, such is no longer the case. Men and women alike are to be baptized and to share in the church's public worship.

About the same time that he wrote to the Galatian Christians, Paul also wrote to Christians in Corinth. In this correspondence he discussed what role women should take in leading worship. His conclusion is clear: women are to keep silent. His reasons for this position, which appear in 1 Corinthians 11:2-16, are confusing. In the earlier part of this discussion Paul uses arguments based on teachings about creation and human nature. In verse 3 he states that there is a "pecking order" in creation. Just as God is Christ's head, so Christ is man's head. And man is woman's head. In verses 4 and 5a Paul makes a second statement, that a man should pray with his head uncovered while a woman should pray with hers covered. In verses 5b and 6 he extends this idea by saying that if a woman leaves off the veil she really should go ahead and shave her head, which would be disgraceful. Paul fails to give any reason for this argument by ridicule. He then restates the hierarchical assertion of verse 3: man is "the image and glory of God; but woman is the glory of man."

Finally in verses 8-10 he gives two reasons to support this claim. The first echoes the Genesis account of creation: that woman was made from man, not man from woman; and therefore she is for man, not he for her. His second reason may have been clear to his readers then but is hard for us to understand now. A woman should wear a veil on her head "because of the angels." There is no explanation. Does he mean good angels or bad ones? Is the veil necessary because angels will assault unprotected women, while leaving men alone? Or is it because women are inherently more sinful than men and therefore more easily tempted? In the teaching of the rabbis of that time, and in later theology, the greater sinfulness of women was one doctrine. Eve had first yielded to temptation, and the later doctrines of the sinfulness of sexuality always placed the blame on women more than on men. Ceremonies for purification after childbirth were prescribed for women, but not for the men who sired the children. It seems likely that this theological point of view was the reason for Paul's system which put women at the bottom of the scale of honor.

To this point in his argument the apostle is consistent even though we have trouble understanding some of the details. In verses 11 and 12, however, he shifts ground and confuses the discussion by denying this system. He now says that they are equal, that man is not superior to woman nor woman superior to man. Here he seems to be implying the position stated so forthrightly in Galatians, that in Christ there is neither male nor female.

Paul has stated two positions which contradict each other. The one is evangelical freedom which clearly calls for equality and the sweeping away of the old law. The other is a doctrine of the subordination of woman to man. Even Paul seems to have recognized the awkwardness of this contradiction because he shifts ground again. In verses 13-16 he grounds his argument on common sense and prevailing custom—judge for yourselves, and this is how we all do it anyway. In this chapter where he discusses the relationship between men and women that is the end of the matter. For Paul it is not theology or Bible, but common sense, secular ideas, and custom that support the subordination of women to men.

In the fourteenth chapter Paul applies this point of view to the conduct of public worship. He says that women should keep silence in church. Such is the custom in all of the churches (1 Corinthians 14:33). The law requires silence (verse 34). It is shameful for them to speak in church (verse 35). If they want to know anything they should ask their husbands at home. Paul's doctrine of subordination of women is based on the old law, on prevailing custom, and on common sense. Yet elsewhere in his writings, he asserts that in Christ the law is set aside and all things are made new. Later writings in the New Testament presume this male leadership, and through the generations the custom has become even more firmly established. Law and ancient custom seem to have won out over the new freedom of the gospel.

To this point I have tried to present the ideas and teachings of the early church concerning its public leaders. But what about today? Who should be the people who preside over the feast of joy now? While it is important to understand the biblical patterns, we have to make conclusions for church life today. Since the New Testament books were written, three developments have taken place. First, the pattern of church leadership has expanded so that several forms now exist. Several doctrines about this subject are present in the church. We cannot simply return to early practice since everything we do is colored by these later developments. The most widespread pattern concentrates responsibility in a group of theologically educated persons, publicly authorized to lead, charged with responsibility to lead worship, preach, preside over communion. These leaders are commonly called ministers, pastors, or priests even though in some churches (like those in the Methodist family) their official title is elder. A second pattern is to commit that kind of leadership-responsibilities to persons of mature character but without special training, who care for the church as unsalaried ministers. A third pattern has grown out of the second. A trained and salaried ministry is joined with the volunteer leaders of the church. In the Christian Church (Disciples of Christ), for example, the normal pattern is to have a board of elders who together are responsible for spiritual oversight in the congregation. Their public leadership is focused at the Lord's Table where they normally are responsible for offering the communion prayer. In addition there is a pastor, well-studied in the Bible and theology, paid by the church, responsi-

66

ble for spiritual and organizational oversight of the congregation.

A second major development that affects contemporary practice is the emergence of new secular conditions. Paul and the writers of the pastoral epistles considered the ideas and practices of their age when they made decisions. We also have to consider our age. The world of Greece and Rome, with its philosophies, religions, and social practices, was the secular realm with which they had to deal. Ours is the world of western civilization, built on the foundation of Greece and Rome but with a superstructure made up of ideas and institutions developed in Europe and transformed by American experience. For example, the form of government is greatly different. So is the pattern of education. The availability of information and methods of communication make our worlds different. Paul could assume certain conditions which we cannot, such as the legality of slavery and the denial of civil rights to women.

A third development is that we have had a long time to think about the meaning of the gospel. Even in the New Testament the disciples showed growth in their understanding. In Peter's sermon on Pentecost the divinity of Jesus is expressed in only a partial manner. ". . . God had made him both Lord and Christ. . ." (Acts 2:36). A generation later the gospel of John begins with a much stronger declaration of Jesus' relationship to God: "In the beginning was the Word, and the Word was with God, and the Word was God. . . And the Word became flesh and dwelt among us, full of grace and truth" (John 1:1, 14). Through the centuries that followed, the church continued to think about and discuss this question, trying to understand its faith. In similar fashion Christians have continued to think about the meaning of Christian freedom and the ways that Christ changes human relationships. The New Testament is like a seed, filled with the power of life, genetically programmed to develop certain kinds of plants. We cannot tell simply by looking at the seed what the plant will be like. Paul's teachings, especially about freedom in Christ, are now growing into the full plant, breaking out of the confining container of the ancient world.

What conclusions can be made for leaders of worship in the church today? With respect to women as leaders of worship, the time has come to replace law by gospel, and an archaic custom with a new one. Common sense calls for different practices now from those of the Graeco-Roman world in which Paul lived. Galatians 3:28, with the insistence upon equality before Christ, must be chosen over 1 Corinthians 14:33-34 which assumes that women are inferior to men. The former passage more clearly reveals the mind of Christ than does the latter.

What this means in practice can be summed up in two statements of policy. The first is that there can be no barrier that keeps women from serving as leader of Word and Sacrament. The call of God comes to women to be ministers and elders just as it comes to men. The church has previously refused to honor that call. The time has come for us to hear and respond to it. There is, however, a second principle which is that we must work energetically and imaginatively to keep a significant number of men in such places. Women often show more faithfulness in carrying out the duties of office than do men. They have traditionally shown skill in church work and maturity in religious life. They could easily become dominant. Yet, men ought not be permitted to fall away from religious leadership. Their consciences should be kept sensitive to the need and the church should continue to elect them to the ministry and to the eldership.

We can draw conclusions concerning the ethical qualifications of those who lead the church. The pastoral epistles especially make it clear that the bishop, elders, and deacons are to be persons whom the community at large respects. Lest there be any uncertainty about what that meant, specific lists of moral qualities were given. Which is more important, the general principle or the list of illustrations for congregations in the ancient world? How should the list be understood, as laws which have to be obeyed or as examples of the kinds of issues to be considered?

In general categories, the list deals with relations to the family, self-control in the use of alcohol and in disputes with other people, and helpfulness toward other people. The list is silent about some moral qualities that are important today, such as honesty, responsible use of money, good citizenship. In order for persons to meet the general principle of being worthy of respect in our world, we have to add some things to the list of particulars and perhaps reduce in importance some of the items from the first century list.

A useful exercise would be to prepare a contemporary list of important qualifications drawing both from those given in the pastoral epistles and those that come from experience today. This revised list could then be used as the basis for selecting ministers and elders today. In this way the intentions of the New Testament writers would probably be more fully realized than if we were to insist upon the use only of the lists published by the church in the ancient world.

Maturity of faith is also necessary for persons who lead the church's public life. There are several ways to understand what this means. One way is the basic set of a person's life. To be Christian, persons must organize their lives around Jesus Christ—trusting his life and message as faithful revelations of God's true life, finding in him release from their sense of guilt, discovering in him purpose and motivation for their moral action. It is especially necessary that leaders of the church's life exhibit this kind of trust in Christ.

Another way of understanding faith is to consider it as knowledge of Christian teaching. Those who lead the church's public life ought to be acquainted with the Bible. This much could be considered as the minimum: (1) knowledge of the main outline of the biblical story, beginning with Abraham and continuing through the life of the early church described in the New Testament; (2) familiarity with the life and teachings of Jesus; (3) acquaintance with some of the best known passages of the Bible, such as the Ten Commandments (Exodus 20:1-17), the Sermon on the Mount (Matthew 5, 6, 7), and the chapter on love (1 Corinthians 13). This kind of scriptural knowledge is within the range of persons who study on their own or in church school classes. All persons who are ordained can be expected to know this much, and elders can develop similar knowledge. Ordained ministers and salaried leaders of the church, of course, rightfully can be expected to know far more. For that reason they ordinarily attend seminary before entering fully into their work in the life of the church.

A further way of understanding maturity of faith for leaders of the church's public life is to define it as stability of character, good judgment, the ability to evaluate conditions and act wisely. These traits of character are what enable persons to serve as shepherds, defending and helping the church.

One final word about the qualifications for leaders of the church is that these three items dealing with manner of life and faith are goals toward which all Christians should strive. Few persons ever achieve the fullness of Christian character, but all of us can strive toward that goal. Those who aspire to the places of leadership should already be well advanced along the way.

A Pattern of Sounds
and Sights

In previous chapters I have talked about the feast of joy as
though it were a structure of actions and words ruled by logic, in
which precision of meaning, exactness of sequence, and
authority of leaders were the major considerations. In the
remaining chapters I want to approach the Lord's Supper from
two other perspectives. In this chapter it is portrayed as an artistic event, a carefully wrought pattern of sounds and sights. In
the next chapter I am discussing what may be the most difficult
part of the subject: how we can enter into the feast of joy

wholeheartedly and jubilantly.

The feast of joy is an artistic event. Meaning is conveyed as much by the shape and artistry of an action as it is by the words and ceremonies themselves. No matter what we say at the Lord's table, for example, its joyful character will be expressed primarily by music and artistic form. Consequently, it follows that if the pattern of sounds and sights is mournful or sluggish, the service will be, too, no matter how much we say about joy and festivity in the common meditation.

There are other reasons for considering the artistic aspects of the feast of joy. One of them is the character of God. In the Bible his glory and majesty are often acclaimed. Solomon built "an exalted house" (1 Kings 8:13) where God could live forever. Other glimpses of worship in the Bible suggest that worship was carried out so as to be harmonious with the divine glory. Since the feast of joy is celebrated for the public honor of God, the effort to make its words and actions consistent with his character is still important for us to do.

Another reason to discuss music and ceremony is the fact that they help a group of people do things together. Marching makes it possible to harness energies and direct them. Music, or at least a rhythmical beating of time, helps people go forward together by channeling emotional power and concentrating physical energies where they are most needed. While worship is a freer act than is a march, similar dynamics also are at work in the feast of joy.

Again, the pattern of music and ceremony accents the service, bringing its most important parts into sharpest focus. A fanfare is an example. The wedding march alerts family and friends to the bride's grand entrance. The moment long awaited has come! Music and ceremony can provide freshness and variety, thus keeping a frequently repeated activity from becoming dull and habitual.

Music and ceremony are closely involved with each other, each influencing the other. In the following analysis, however, I am trying to deal with them separately, first music and then ceremony. My purpose is not to lay down rules nor is it to establish uniform practice. Rather, it is for the purpose of suggesting by example how the feast of joy can be given an artistic form that is fitting to its own nature.

The most valuable form of music in worship is congregational song. One of its functions in the feast of joy is to serve as border to the service, marking its beginning and its ending. This function is especially clear when the communion hymn is divided, part of it being sung at the beginning of communion and part at the end. A more common practice is for one hymn to be used at the beginning of the Lord's Supper, marking the transition into communion and often providing the occasion for the leaders to take their places at the table. Another function of congregational song is to be the means for the people to do their part in the service. In the offering, for example, they place their gifts in the trays, but then comes the presentation and placing of those gifts on the table. At this point it is common practice for the congregation to stand and sing a hymn which becomes the instrument by which they say "this action belongs to us." Another place where the congregation uses song as the instrument for its participation is the middle of the communion prayer. In some traditions there is the exclamation of joy: "Holy, holy, holy, Lord God of hosts; heaven and earth are full of your glory." This is for all to proclaim; and it works best when it can be sung rather than said.

In such places as these the musical material must be suitable and singable. Suitable means that both words and melody fit the occasion. Singable means that the people can handle the song; and that they know it well enough to sing it out. It is possible, however, for the music of a service to be repeated so often that it bores the people instead of stimulating them to their worship of God. In many places, this fate has overtaken the Gloria Patri and the Doxology. Ministers and musicians can deal with this problem by introducing other texts and tunes, some of which may be single stanzas of hymns. Instead of the Gloria Patri, for example, the congregation could sing stanza five of "As the Sun Doth Daily Rise":

> Praise we, with the heavenly host,
> Father, Son, and Holy Ghost;
> Thee would we with one accord
> Praise and magnify, O Lord! Amen.

Or stanza three from "Of the Father's Love Begotten":

> Christ, to thee with God the Father,
> And, O Holy Ghost, to thee,
> Hymn and chant and high thanksgiving,
> And unwearied praises be:
> Honor, glory, and dominion,
> And eternal victory
> Evermore and evermore. Amen.

Instead of the Doxology, a congregation could use the last stanza of "Now Thank We All Our God":

All praise and thanks to God
The Father now be given,
The Son, and him who reigns
With them in highest heaven,
The one eternal God,
Whom earth and heaven adore,
For thus it was, is now,
And shall be evermore. Amen.

The third function of congregational song is to set the devotional tone for the service. Is communion to be joyous or penitential, exuberant or restrained? Although the language used and the manner of the leaders will do much toward establishing the chosen quality, the music more quickly and effectively does so, especially when the congregation does the singing. When "Crown Him with Many Crowns" is used as the communion hymn, the service takes on a strong, triumphant tone, quite different from that established by "Bread of the Word in Mercy Broken." Both hymns are suitable for communion, both moods appropriate, but the two results are strikingly different. In some churches the congregation sings a hymn while the communion elements are being distributed. The effect can be very strong, much stronger than is the quiet instrumental music more often played at this time. The hymn chosen for use at this time in the service has an especially strong impact upon the emotional tone of the feast.

Another form of music in the service is that sung by choir or solo voices. One of its major functions is to assist the congregation in doing its part of the service. By rehearsing new or difficult hymns, the choir can lead the congregation in its singing. Some hymns are beyond the congregation's ability; but the choir can sing the stanzas while the people sing the choruses.

Choral music by select groups also helps to set the devotional tone of a service. This function is possible because a wider range of music is available to the choir than to the congregation. The choir rehearses, submits to the director's musical discipline, and grows in its ability to sing. It is thus more flexible than is the congregation. Music sung by select groups is especially useful during the portion of the service when the elements are being distributed. As soon as the bread has been broken, a choral meditation upon the meaning of the feast of joy repeats the ideas previously expressed and provides the emotional tone which the bare, spoken words do not possess. The ancient text of the hymn "Holy Communion" by Thomas Aquinas is one example of what the choir could sing.

Humbly I adore thee, Verity unseen.
Who thy glory hidest 'neath these shadows mean;
Lo, to thee surrendered, my whole heart is bowed,
Tranced as it beholds thee, shrined within the cloud.

A second example, this more vigorous in character, is "At the Name of Jesus."

At the name of Jesus Every knee shall bow,
Every tongue confess him King of glory now;
'Tis the Father's pleasure We should call him Lord,
Who from the beginning Was the mighty word.

Still another example of a hymn for the choir to sing at this point in the service is "Fairest Lord Jesus."

Instrumental music also highlights congregational song and assists the work done by choirs or soloists. In its own right it too is useful in setting the tone for a service.

Although most congregations use music in communion, many of them do so in such a way that the service is bland and dull, not at all consistent with the powerful ideas that are expressed in communion. Some suggestions can be given for using music more effectively.

First, let the texts of hymns deal explicitly with the basic meanings of the Lord's Supper. Some texts are vague, as can be illustrated by the hymn "Bread of the World, In Mercy Broken":

Bread of the world, in mercy broken,
Wine of the soul, in mercy shed.

It is hard to figure out what is being said. In contrast, there is the vivid language of "Here At Thy Table, Lord":

Here at thy table, Lord, we meet
To feed on food divine:
Thy body is the bread we eat,
Thy precious blood the wine.

Or this, in "Jesus Christ, Our Blessed Savior":
Jesus Christ, our blessed Savior,
Shows the Father's love forever;
By his bitter grief and cruel pain
He purges us from every stain.

The mid-century sentimentality that avoided the direct language of both the Bible and classical liturgies is best put behind us in favor of language that expresses strong ideas and emotions.

Let the tunes be vigorous and strong. Again, there has been sentimentality at work in the selection of the bland and dull

74

tunes used at communion time. Examples are "Break Thou the Bread of Life" and the Mendelssohn tune "Consolation" to which we commonly sing "Here, O my Lord, I see thee face to face." Far more spirited is the tune "Donne Secours" with words like:

O Lord and Savior, as we kneel before thee,
Taking from thee by faith the bread of life.

An exciting hymn for use at communion is "Come, Christians, join to sing," set to Madrid, perhaps using tambourines or other percussion instruments during the "Alleluia! Amen!" at the end of each line.

When this kind of strong, vigorous music is introduced at communion, however, there may be objections from the people of the congregation. One is that they no longer have time for personal meditation. The other is that communion is supposed to be a quiet time. These two objections lead me to the third and fourth suggestions.

Third, let there be time in every communion service when people can meditate quietly. One of the major values of the Lord's Supper is that it does provide periods of quietness when persons can carry out their own meditations and prayers. They experience the sense of closeness to God which does not come to them at other times in the service. When the music becomes too strong, it demands their attention. They no longer can use it to screen out distractions so that they can think about God; instead the music itself becomes a distraction. To honor their desire for time to meditate, there needs to be an alternation of strong, attention-demanding music and other sounds that are docile in character. The congregational song used to frame the service should be strong, as should be the music used as part of the offering. Choral music sung during communion should be planned so that there is also time for persons to pray without having to contend with song. Sometimes the song can be quiet, reinforcing the desire to meditate. Or it can be more demanding when other time for meditation is provided.

These times for meditation need to come at the same point in the service week after week. We are creatures of habit and worship becomes reflexive. We can more easily pray at the times when we have become conditioned for praying than we can at other times.

Fourth, let there be variety over the course of the year. The sequence of major parts provides continuity. They should stay the same and the sequence be unchanged. The words and music provide the variety. They can and should change over the course

75

of time. In order to be useful, however, the changes should be made so that the people experience the feeling of freshness and interest. Very little that is good is accomplished if the people are never aware of change or if the changes confuse and irritate them.

One way of accomplishing change is to plan the communion service as a unit for each season of the Christian year. The mood of that season could be used to select the music and shape the text of prayers and congregational meditations. Perhaps one hymn could be used throughout the season so that people in the congregation become familiar with it. During Advent, for example, the communion hymn might be "Let all mortal flesh keep silence." During Epiphany it might be something much different like "Come, Christians, Join to Sing." Lent is another somber period and the hymn might be "O Sacred Head, Now Wounded." Then comes the jubilation of Easter and a hymn like "Deck Thyself, My Soul, with Gladness," would be a possibility. The result could be that communion, often one of the dullest parts of the Sunday service, could become one of the brightest.

The twin to music is ceremony, the movements, gestures, and visual symbols that are used to conduct the service. The place to begin the consideration of ceremony is with architecture and the physical elements of the Lord's Supper. Although the theological requirements are simple—a table, bread, and the cup—the ceremonial requirements are more complex. The table should be easily seen by the people of the congregation, large enough to hold the bread, wine, and money trays, and located so that movements are easy and graceful. One of the most common faults in church design is that the table is crowded, therefore making the movements of leaders and congregation difficult. There should be room for minister and elders to stand near the table, and for the deacons to receive their trays and present the offerings. Since the congregation should be able to hear what is said at the table, some attention should be given to acoustics. If it is necessary to amplify voices, the microphones should be designed, placed, and used so as not to detract from the service.

The table should be set so that it is visually strong. The older tradition was to cover it with a spotless linen cloth and to cover the elements similarly. It is doubtful that other forms of adornment surpass this in visual appeal. When crosses and candles are used, care should be taken lest the table look cluttered and crowded.

What kind of bread and "fruit of the vine" should be used? There is good reason to return to ancient practice and the use of leavened bread in communion. It looks like bread so that the symbolism is clear to people in the congregation. It can be broken in their presence. The loaf should be chosen with the size of the congregation in mind. It doesn't take very much to provide the communion needs for a good sized group. A regular dinner roll, for example, will probably be enough for a congregation of 50 or more persons. If a much larger loaf is brought to the table, the leader of the service could break off a small portion prior to the communion prayer, using that for the communion bread proper. The larger "unblessed" loaf could then be distributed after the service during the fellowship time. When a loaf is used in the ceremony at the table, it should be the communion bread for someone—at least for the leaders of the service.

Although the original communion drink was fermented wine, pasteurized grape juice came into widespread use in the latter part of the nineteenth century. Some congregations have returned to using wine. The continuation of ideas formed during the temperance movement and new concerns growing out of the dangers of alcoholism make it unlikely, however, that there will be a widespread return to the use of fermented wine. Because of interests in hygiene, congregations which have adopted the use of individual cups are not likely to return to the use of the single chalice.

Some gestures ought to be seen by the congregation. The setting of the table with the gifts, or the uncovering of them, the pouring of the wine, the breaking of the bread are movements which should be made openly and gracefully. If words are spoken at the same time, the leaders should commit them to memory or in some other way be freed from holding a book so that their hands are free to make the gestures.

In most American protestant churches the custom is for people to bow their heads and close their eyes when praying. Thus, there is little need for gestures during the communion prayer. When the text is uniform, as in some traditions, this text will increasingly be memorized. In traditions like the Christian Church (Disciples of Christ) the text will change from week to week. In these instances, especially, it is desirable that the prayer be thought about in advance. Often it is written down and the leader holds the text while leading in prayer.

I want to close this chapter by reaffirming its character: It is meant to suggest possibilities rather than to lay down rules. In each congregation there are people with artistic skill and imagination who can design the pattern of sights and sounds. The task is important, challenging, always present. Our biblical

warrant is this refrain from Psalm 147:
>Praise the Lord!
>For it is good to sing praises to our God;
>>for he is gracious, and a song of praise is seemly.

8

All Things Are Ready!
Come to the Feast

When the people in charge say that it's time to eat, we all
crowd around the picnic tables. While the adults go through
their "you first" politeness game, the kids grab up their plates
and scoop up their food. By then all of the rest are in line and
ready to fill their plates. It is inconceivable that we go to a picnic
and refuse to eat. What is almost as hard to imagine is turning
down a chance to go to the festive meal. When the promise is
congenial people, good food, and a good time, we are likely to
accept the invitation.

"All things are ready," a hymn announces, "come to the feast. Come, for the doors are open wide." Yet we resist the invitation and even when we come to the feast of joy we sometimes refuse to share in the bread and wine. We are very much like the people whom Jesus described in a parable (Matthew 22:1-10; Luke 14:16-24). A rich man planned a banquet and invited many guests. When preparations were complete, he sent his servants out, saying: "Come, for all is ready." Instead of coming, they stayed away for several reasons, business and personal. The man was angered and sent his servants out a second time with commands to bring in "the poor and maimed and blind and lame."

Non-attendance is a fact that has to be reckoned with. People today stay away from the feast of joy because they have other things to do, some of which are caused by business or employment. Many people have jobs that occupy them during church hours. And many others have home work—school assignments, things they didn't have time to do during their regular working hours, or the endless chores of maintaining a household. Frequently, what keeps us away from the feast of joy is some kind of personal activity. We want to sleep in or sit around reading the paper. There are personal recreations or entertainments, or family activities, to attract our attention.

Non-participation is also a fact with respect to the Lord's Supper. Sometimes persons refuse to eat and drink the feat of joy even though they are present in the service. Some feel that they are unworthy, because of some specific act or because of a more generalized sense of guilt. Some refuse to participate because they don't feel like it today. They are bored by the service or distracted by something else. Some do not share in the meal because they don't know what to do with the quiet period. Not knowing what to think about, they find it difficult to use the feast of joy as a time of genuine communion with God or with anyone else.

Some people do not participate because they feel that there is a conflict between the gentle religious ritual and the harsh life that people are forced to live outside of the safety of church walls and ceremonies. Yearning for greater consistency between their religious life and their secular, they tend to pull away from the ceremonies of religion.

This double condition of non-attendance and non-participation reveals three issues with which this chapter deals: the interaction of ecclesiastical processes and secular patterns, the nature of religious motivation, and the relationship of personal worth and religious practice.

While the questions of authority and worthiness are religious, dealing with inner experience, the third question, is functional. It deals with the relation of church life and secular life. One reason for non-participation in the feast of joy is the mismatching of the patterns of life inside the church and outside. Here it is possible to take one of three positions.

One is that the church is always right and its patterns are to be dominant. Should there be conflict with secular patterns, they should change while the church remains the same. The most uncompromising example of this approach to the problem is the way of life among Amish who have frozen a particular style of culture and civilization. By means of a complex set of practices, they maintain family and community life in virtual isolation from the main pattern of American society. Their refusal to use electricity and automobiles is a sign of their determination to hold off the corrupting influences of secularity. Although the majority of Christians have lived more easily with secular culture than this, there has until recently been a protection of the church's basic schedule. On Sundays only the church was open and all other organizations were closed. In many communities there was a serious effort extended to reserve one evening a week for church meetings, with school functions at least closed down for that time. This kind of protection has broken down, and everyone can now choose other things to do over going to church. Yet the argument can still be advanced that the serious Christian will refuse to choose secular activities over the religious. Some will obey that guideline however strong the temptation is to do something else.

This point of view, however, is not likely to prevail. Secular life is not to be spurned, nor is any one pattern of church activity to be so highly valued that it is always to be kept unchanged. While a few Christians may be heroic enough to choose a specific church way over society's way, the rank of heroes will shrink as the conflict grows stronger. The greater number will adapt the patterns of the church so that its objectives are maintained however the secular organizations change their shape.

Another position is to assume that the pattern of public life is always to be accepted and that church life must be adapted so that it fits. Most people may say that they don't like it this way, that they would prefer that the church be left free to maintain its schedule. Yet they find the pattern of secular life to be far more than they can overcome and therefore they accept the inevitability of change in the church's patterns. If churchly life is to continue, however, those responsible for it have to keep working. Adapting implies that old activities will be reshaped to fit new circumstances, and that requires imagination and hard work. What easily happens, however, is that adaptation is accomplished only by curtailment. When it became difficult to maintain midweek and Sunday evening services, for example, a great many churches simply dropped them and failed to develop any new ways of achieving similar goals of teaching and nurturing the life of congregations and Christians. Another problem is that however the congregation deals with the problem, individuals respond by dropping some aspect of their involvement in the church, participating only in secular activities. The results for their faith and for the church would be disastrous.

An adequate position will both acknowledge the overwhelming power of secular life and work at preserving the chief values and functions of traditional forms of church life. One example is the changed definition of the Sunday Mass for Roman Catholics. There has always been the requirement that Catholics attend Mass each Sunday and a tightly packed schedule of services on Sunday mornings provided a fairly wide choice of times. In the post-Vatican II period, however, that church acknowledged that there are problems with that limitation of time. By broadening the definition of Sunday and revising the discipline of fasting prior to communion, the church could schedule the Sunday service for Saturday and Sunday evenings as well as for Sunday mornings. While the Sunday obligation was preserved as necessary for catholic Christians, the increased secularization of Sunday was also accepted as a fact of contemporary life.

In order to make this kind of adaptation, however, the church has to be clear as to what is necessary in order for its life to be maintained. Although my own convictions have already been presented throughout this book, I want to draw this topic to a close by summarizing them.

(1) Sunday will continue to be the regular time for Christians to meet. By this statement I mean that the weekly assembly is still necessary and that the first day—the Lord's Day—is the time. Current patterns may change drastically. Yet even if time is completely secularized, the spiritual health of Christians requires that they devise effective ways of assembling on what can be called the first day of the week. Although I cannot forecast what will happen in the future, I suspect that we will have to find ways of spending less time on Sunday mornings doing what needs to be done. People are less and less ready to devote the full morning to church activities.

(2) The Bible is the beginning point of conversation for this weekly gathering. It is our book, and it binds us to God and to the

82

historic Christian faith as nothing else can do. The Bible needs to be read publicly, preached, and learned by the people.

(3) The feast of joy portrays the foundations of our faith and deepens our experience of it. Although other ways of accomplishing these functions might have developed, the fact is that the Lord's Supper is the one that did arise. I see no way that some new ritual symbol could now take its place.

The second issue deals with motivation for the Christian life and is nicely stated in a column dealing with the second Vatican Council. The writer said that while the council may have been good Christianity, it certainly was bad politics because it seemed to make it easier to leave the church and less urgent to join. And then he says: "Conscience now sat on the throne beside authority, and the most obvious public results of the council were the resignation of many priests from their office, a falling off in vocations and conversions, and a new sort of doubt about the validity of some of the church's commands. . ." (Patrick O'Donovan, *Indianapolis Star,* November 8, 1975, p. 10).What kind of motivation is strong enough to make us do what we ought to do? Is it *authority?* Some law or officer who has the power to force us to do its bidding? Or is it *conscience?* A conviction about truth that motivates us from the inside?

Some schools operate on the honor system, which is a way of giving exams which assumes that everyone is honest and honorable. Since no one would ever think of cheating, the instructor hands out the exam and then leaves, coming back only to collect the blue books at the end of the hour. In most schools, however, this form of conscience doesn't work. Only authority, a teacher or proctor right there in the classroom, is enough. This same conflict can be found at work where some people stay on the job because of self-esteem, the intrinsic interest of the work, or because they believe that it is right to put in a good day's work. Yet at the same time we have to bother with time clocks, bells and recorded music during coffee breaks, supervisors, and inspectors. Public appeals may be made to conscience; but authority stands close by waiting to enforce its will upon even the most unwilling.

This same conflict takes place in the religious life. Why do we serve God? What makes us live the good life? Why do we struggle against sin with all of its allures, or keep working at unpleasant tasks? Is it because of conscience, a deep inner voice that urges us onward? Or is it fear of hell and lust for heaven?

There is much to be said in favor of religion which enthrones authority. The Bible is full of it: the law of Moses, the ten commandments, the jealous God who sends plagues to Egypt and crushes the disobedient nation of Israel. Calvin's form of the reformation, with its emphasis upon predestinarianism and duty, has been foremost in populating and activating post-reformation Christendom. Even now, strict forms of Christianity seem to be prospering more than the freer forms. Religion that gives us no choice seems to work. It is neat and clear. The laws are there and obedience can be measured; no ambiguity, no uncertainty, no gray areas where action depends upon circumstance. Religion with authority on the throne takes human nature seriously. It knows that we are sinners, incapable of saving ourselves, or even of doing what we want to do. And so it supports us with rules, challenges us with promised rewards, and keeps us at it with threats of punishment should we slack off.

Yet religion with conscience on the throne has much in its favor. The biblical record moves from authority to conscience, from law to love, from commandment to grace. Jesus sets aside the authoritarian religion, calling us to a higher life of love and mercy. He leads us to realize that the Old Testament view of God is incomplete. God is creator, powerful Lord of the universe. Yet his preference is loving service rather than fearful obedience. He wins his way by persuasion rather than by force. Conscience is a more mature form of motivation than is authority. The happier kind of home is not the one marked by command and force, but the one where people do the right things because they want to. The same is true for the religious life. It is better to be good because one wants to be than because one has to be.

Unfortunately, we always have to reckon with the fact of our own human sinfulness. We are proud, self-centered, lovers of pleasure, insensitive, cruel. Passion more than rationality rules our conduct. Perhaps that is why authority often works better in religion than does conscience. Yet I still want conscience on the throne in my own life. I want to participate in churches that depend upon conscience with its idealism rather than upon authority with its hard view of human life. But if conscience is to work, there are two things which must take place.

The first of them is to strengthen the center which gives conscience its character. There has to be some clear focus to life, some magnetic pole to which a person's internal compass can point. Let's change the figure. In our bodies certain glands send out their hormones, thus influencing everything that our minds and bodies do. If the glands are working well, our bodies work well, too; but let the glands malfunction, and everything else is upset.

The center for the Christian life, our religious magnetic pole, that spiritual gland controlling everything, is all summed up in our confession of faith: Jesus Christ, Lord and Savior. In order for conscience to be effective, this affirmation must be proclaimed and established in the heart and mind of every believer. For a Christian to put conscience on the throne does not mean "I'll do what I think is right." Rather, it means "I'll do what my Lord and Savior wants me to do."

One purpose of worship is to portray this center of conscience, to invite people to order their lives accordingly, and to keep that center strong. All of the service helps. Scripture is the cradle that holds Jesus, the sermon is the proclamation of his presence and power, hymns and prayers express our love for him. Most important is the feast of joy because the dramatic actions here show him most fully. We remember his ministry, share in his death, experience his risen presence. And we are shamed because of our sin and renewed in our desire to follow him.

We must strengthen the center; but we must also build up some supports that help conscience even when it is weak. Because of sin we all are impaired, unable to act in the full strength of Christian maturity. When a person is seriously injured it often is necessary to give him or her some mechanical supports: a sling to hold a broken arm, a brace on a bad back, a pace maker to help the heart beat regularly, a walker to assist in walking. The mechanical assist lets a person help himself despite the damaged part. Because conscience is flawed, it needs braces, a group of half-laws or practical guidelines that work even when the spirit is weak. We need these half-laws to support our relations with family and close friends. We depend upon them to keep us going in school, and work, and public life. We need pace makers for our participation in the church.

Although I have some half-laws for my own life, there is little value in pushing them off on other people. Instead of imitating some one else, each Christian will advance more quickly in the life of faith by developing his or her own set of guidelines, thus dealing effectively with the question of motivation.

Feelings of unworthiness at the Lord's Table take two forms, and here I turn to the third issue. Some Christians hesitate to take communion because they feel themselves unfit to share in this holy meal. When asked to be leaders of the service, other persons hold back because they are convinced that they are too immature in their Christian lives to exercise public responsibility in the church.

Each of these attitudes is based on a true perception of our human condition. We do fall short—of God's expectations for us, of the hopes of family and friends, and of our own best desires. When they had sinned, Adam and Eve hid from God instead of meeting him as had been their custom. And so do we. Recognizing our sin, we quail at the thought of appearing before God.

Yet this feeling of unworthiness to share in the feast of joy can quickly lead to two untrue and unfortunate mistakes. One of them is the misunderstanding of the basis for our relationship to God. Always we are able to stand in his presence because of his mercy and love, never because of our goodness, no matter how good we are. An ancient man correctly stated our self-understanding (Psalm 130:3-4).

> If thou, O Lord, shouldst mark iniquities,
> > Lord, who could stand?

He then takes the step that we may forget.

> But there is forgiveness with thee,
> > that thou mayest be feared.

This statement of divine forgiveness is followed by a proclamation of hope (Psalm 130:7).

> O Israel, hope in the Lord!
> > For with the Lord there is steadfast love,
> > and with him is plenteous redemption.

This same attitude is expressed in a devotional sentence which some churches include in the communion service. They borrow the words spoken to Jesus by a centurion in Capernaum: "Lord, I am not worthy to have you come under my roof; but only say the word, and my servant will be healed" (Matthew 8:8). As appropriate for the Lord's Supper, this sentence acknowledges both our recognition of sin and our knowledge that God's love is greater than our weakness.

This sentence also helps correct the second mistake that we are inclined to make, which is to misunderstand the reason why the Lord gave us this meal. Rather than a reward for the perfect, it is an event set up for those who need help. Another classical communion devotion expresses this attitude.

> Jesus, Lamb of God:
> > have mercy on us.
> Jesus, bearer of our sins:
> > have mercy on us.
> Jesus, redeemer of the world:
> > give us your peace.

In this prayer, which has been recited for some 1,100 years, Christians confess their sinfulness. Yet they also reveal their hope that Jesus will show his mercy, carry their sins on his own shoulders, and give them peace.

When these two mistaken ideas are corrected, our fear of sharing the meal and serving at the table is made over into a new and constructive attitude. It is a combination of modesty and boldness. God loves us because he chose to. Therefore, we have no right to boast of our own achievements nor to act as though we deserve any good thing that happens in our religious life. Yet, God calls on us to live in the reality of our forgiven state—to rejoice, to try to live as new creatures, to declare abroad his love and his will. We therefore can share the bread and wine. And we can legitimately take up responsibilities for leading the service. Our Lord Jesus Christ invites us and offers himself to be our helper.

9

A Few Words about the Future

The service of the Lord's Supper has always been part of the church's life. For 2000 years Christians have met around the table, there met Jesus and each other, there found power for life. For two millenia poets have described the Lord's Supper, musicians have composed for it, theologians have defined it, church people have prepared bread and wine for it. Many people have died because of their beliefs about this sacrament. Something so deeply ingrained in the church's life will not easily disappear.

Furthermore, the Lord's Supper uses symbolic material that is universal, spreading across time and around the world. It is a meal, one of the most elemental of all human actions. Because eating is so familiar, we don't have to think about the action itself; it can carry special meanings. We celebrate birthdays with a meal, reunions with a meal, anniversaries with a meal. The Lord's Supper, following Old Testament precedent, uses a meal to convey religious meanings. So long as human beings break bread together, the symbolism of the feast of joy will be understandable and capable of carrying the meanings I have talked about in these pages.

We are in a period of time when the cultural dominance of the church is fading. Fewer people are Christian than once was the case. Despite this decline, there still are large numbers of people, many of them young, who seek to follow Jesus. For those who do, the Lord's Supper is going to be there waiting for them.

I have written this book from the view point of the free prayer approach to worship which I also believe will continue. It is an ancient practice. It is deeply ingrained in the American spirit. It works, and this despite the carelessness with which it has often been done.

There will, however, be changes in the coming years. Perhaps most important will be the interaction with the thought and practice of the secular world. The church has always been involved with the culture and civilization in which it is placed. In the ancient world it learned Greek and then Latin. In later times the church adopted the philosophy of Aristotle to explain the mystery of the Lord's Supper. New languages have been used—English, Chinese, Bantu. New forms of music have been brought into worship. This process will continue, calling upon each generation to make a fresh blending of its past experience and its new.

A second development will be cross fertilization with other traditions. During recent years, and especially since the second Vatican Council, Christians have been rediscovering each other. Baptists and Catholics are getting acquainted, Lutherans and Disciples, Presbyterians and Pentecostals. Our several ways of worship are being altered by these encounters. Churches like the Episcopal Church, with formal and prescribed services of worship, are developing freer patterns. At the same time, churches that have used extempore or free prayer have moved toward the occasional use of materials from other traditions. There still are clear family traits. Lutherans are still recognizable and so are the other traditions. The sharp edges, however, have been blunted and we can more readily move from one pattern to another.

Another development will be a more widely recognized consensus concerning the meaning of the Lord's Supper. This subject has been debated heatedly through the centuries, causing much pain and suffering. The meaning of this sacrament has been one of the chief means of distinguishing between Catholics, Lutherans, Disciples, and all of the rest. We are now discovering a surprising body of agreement, especially in the conviction that at the Lord's Table we meet Jesus our Lord and Savior. There still are sharp differences in our efforts to explain how this all is possible. Yet even here theologians increasingly are drawing upon a common stock of ideas and authorities in their efforts to interpret what happens when we go to communion. I expect this movement toward theological consensus to continue.

The feast of joy is likely to move even closer to the center of the church's life. During the middle portion of this century, Sunday School, fellowship activities, and other aspects of church program were expanded. Church buildings were enlarged to keep pace. This organizational and educational growth has slacked off. The church is once again becoming a community that meets to worship more than to do these other things. Furthermore, when Christians gather to worship, they want the words and ceremonies to work—to connect them to God. They want preaching to make a difference and sacramental acts to communicate power. The feast of joy does this; it provides a connecting link with God and the strength for life that he promises.

Because the feast of joy will continue, Christian men and women will be enlisted to plan and lead this service of worship. Paul's exhortation is to all such persons: ". . . Be steadfast, immovable, always abounding in the work of the Lord, knowing that in the Lord your labor is not in vain" (1 Corinthians 15:58).

PART TWO

The Language of the Lord's Supper— Some Examples

One of the most demanding responsibilities for leaders of worship is to choose the right words to say in the service next Sunday. It is hard enough to be ready when the church has already provided a worship book with most of the necessary prayers and other materials. In churches like my own the work is even more difficult. With the Bible and hymnal their chief sources, and the Holy Spirit their inspiration, the appointed leaders prepare and lead calls to worship, invitations, blessings, devotions, and prayers.

Part two of this book contains examples of what can be said. There are selections from the Bible adapted for use in the service, a few materials selected from service books, and statements and prayers that I have written. Although this collection is too limited to serve as a service book for any length of time, I have arranged it so that ministers and elders could for a while use it as a manual for conducting the Lord's Supper. These materials can also be used as the basis for study and the stimulus for drafting one's own materials.

Some of these prayers and devotional elements have accumulated during recent years in my own service as elder or minister at the table. Others, especially the communion meditations, were written for this book. The following guidelines have been used:

1) These materials are to be serviceable in congregations of the free tradition, including those where the communion service is led by elders who have not had theological training.

2) As much as possible, they are to be consistent with theological understandings of worship embraced by contemporary Christianity.

3) They are to be faithful to New Testament ideas concerning the meaning of the Lord's Supper.

4) They are to be shaped by biblical language and contemporary English style.

I have arranged the materials into six groups, some of which are subdivided. At the beginning of each group there are a few sentences explaining the function of the materials in that section.

10

The Words of Institution

Three of the gospels and 1 Corinthians recount the establishing of the Lord's Supper. Jesus is described as taking up the bread, giving thanks to God, breaking it, and giving it to the disciples. In similar manner he handles the cup. Even in their biblical form these passages give the impression that they had long been used in the regular worship of Christians. There is other non-biblical evidence that from ancient times these words of institution were part of the service. In our own time this language continues to be used, either in one of the New Testament forms or in a combination of two or more of them.

There are three places in the communion service where the words of institution are likely to occur—as part of the approach to the table, in the text of the communion prayer, and as part of the breaking of bread prior to the distribution to the congregation.

When used in the approach to the table, these words are sometimes called the warrant, meaning that they state the authority by which the church conducts this ceremonial meal. It is done in the name and by the authority of Jesus himself, who first gave it a meaning that was to be remembered each time the meal is eaten.

The second place for the words of institution is in the text of the prayer itself. From as early as the fourth century they have appeared here and that has been their location in most prayer book orders of the Lord's Supper. In services where the words of institution are part of the prayer, they constitute the major means of recalling Jesus and his sacrifice for his people. In the Roman Catholic Church, and to a lesser degree in Lutheran and Episcopal Churches, these words are mandatory as part of the prayer, for God's action in the Lord's Supper is believed to be sharply focused in them. Whatever transformation he makes in the elements and in the worshipers is believed to be conditioned by these words of institution.

A third placement is in the ceremony of the breaking of the bread following the prayer. While saying the part of the text that refers to the bread, the leader takes up the loaf and breaks it. While referring to the cup, the leader either pours wine from a pitcher into a chalice or takes up the vessel. Although the breaking of bread can be done silently, or accompanied by other words, the dramatic intensity when the words of institution are used is especially strong.

The words can be used as they appear in one of the biblical texts. Or a combination of them can be developed and used. When they appear in either the first or third position (before the prayer or after it), they are spoken to the congregation. In such a case the dramatic power is increased when the leader has committed them to memory and therefore does not need to read them from the service book.

1. Now as they were eating,
   Jesus took bread and blessed,
   and broke it, and gave it to the Disciples
   and said,

"Take, eat; this is my body."
And he took a cup,
and when he had given thanks
he gave it to them, saying,
"Drink of it, all of you;
for this is my blood of the covenant,
which is poured out for many for the
  forgiveness of sins."
  (Matthew 26:26-28)

2. And as they were eating,
he took bread, and blessed,
and broke it, and gave it to them,
and said,
"Take; this is my body."
And he took a cup,
and when he had given thanks
he gave it to them, and they
all drank of it.
And he said to them,
"This is my blood of the covenant,
which is poured out for many."
  (Mark 14:22-24)

3. And he took a cup,
and when he had given thanks he said,
"Take this, and divide it among yourselves;
for I tell you that from now on I shall not drink
of the fruit of the vine until the kingdom
of God comes."
And he took bread, and when he had given thanks
he broke it and gave it to them, saying,
"This is my body."
  (Luke 22:17-20)

4. The Lord Jesus on the night when he was betrayed
took bread, and when he had given thanks,
he broke it, and said,
"This is my body which is broken for you.
Do this in remembrance of me."
In the same way also the cup,

after supper, saying,
"This cup is the new covenant in my blood.
Do this, as often as you drink it,
in remembrance of me."
(1 Corinthians 11:23-25)

These words and actions of Jesus have been cast into slightly different forms in contemporary services of worship. Among them are the following.

5. On the night he was betrayed,
   he took the bread, said the blessing,
   broke the bread, and gave it to his friends,
   and said, "Take, eat:
   This is my Body, which is given for you.
   Do this for the remembrance of me."
   After supper, he took the cup of wine, gave thanks,
   and said, "Drink this, all of you
   This is my Blood of the new Covenant,
   which is poured out for you and for many
   for the forgiveness of sins.
   Whenever you drink, do this for the remembrance of me.
   (The Draft Proposed Book of Common Prayer, p. 373)

6. At supper the night he was betrayed,
   our Lord Jesus took some bread in his hands;
   and then, when he had given thanks to you,
   he broke it and he gave it to his friends.
   And he said, "Take this, and eat it:
   This is my body; it is given for you:
   Do this to remember me."
   After supper he took a cup of wine
   and after giving thanks, he gave it to them.
   And he said, "Drink from this, all of you:
   This cup is God's new covenant in my blood
   which is poured out for you and for all mankind
   for the forgiveness of sins.
   Whenever you drink from now on,
   do this to remember me."
   (Contemporary Worship #2, p. 15)

The Approach

All of the materials in this section have one purpose: to introduce the service of the Lord's Supper. There are several ways to begin a service. By reading *scripture sentences* the leaders anchor the service in biblical language and imply one or more meanings of the Lord's Supper. This approach to the service suggests what is to take place, making use of previous experience and the insight conveyed by the words and actions that follow. *Invitations to the table* are explicit and direct, bidding the people to make ready for what follows. *Communion meditations* are expanded invitations in which a leader states briefly some idea appropriate to the Lord's Supper.

One of the main principles in this manual, discussed in chapter four, is that the offering occurs at the beginning of the Lord's Supper. The materials in this section are written or selected in harmony with this principle.

Scripture Sentences

1. Let the word of Christ dwell in you richly, as you teach and admonish one another in all wisdom, and as you sing psalms and hymns and spiritual songs with thankfulness in your hearts to God. And whatever you do, in word or in deed, do everything in the name of the Lord Jesus giving thanks to God the Father through him. (Colossians 3:16-17)

2. And I heard every creature in heaven and on earth and under the earth and in the sea, and all therein, saying, "To him who sits upon the throne and to the lamb be blessing and honor and glory and might for ever and ever!" And the four living creatures said, "Amen!" and the elders fell down and worshiped. (Revelation 5:13-14)

3. Since . . . we have a great high priest who has passed through the heavens, Jesus, the Son of God, let us hold fast our confession. For we have not a high priest who is unable to sympathize with our weaknesses, but one who in every respect has been tempted as we are, yet without sin(ning). Let us then with confidence draw near to the throne of grace, that we may receive mercy and find grace to help in time of need. (Hebrews 4:14-16)

4. Great indeed, we confess, is the mystery of our religion:
   He was manifested in the flesh,
   vindicated in the Spirit,
       seen by angels,
   preached among the nations,
   believed on in the world,
       taken up in glory. (1 Timothy 3:16)

5. But now in Christ Jesus you who once were far off have been brought near in the blood of Christ. . . . For through him we both have access in one Spirit to the Father. So then you are no longer strangers and sojourners, but you are fellow citizens with the saints and members of the household of God, built upon the foundation of the apostles and prophets,

Christ Jesus himself being the chief cornerstone. (Ephesians 2:13, 18-20)

6. That which was from the beginning, which we have heard, which we have seen with our eyes, which we have looked upon and touched with our hands, concerning the word of life . . . we proclaim also to you, so that you may have fellowship with us; and our fellowship is with the Father and with his Son Jesus Christ. (1 John 1:1, 3)

7. The cup of blessing which we bless, is it not a participation in the blood of Christ? The bread which we break, is it not a participation in the body of Christ? Because there is one loaf, we who are many are one body, for we all partake of the same loaf. (1 Corinthians 10:16-17)

8. Then I looked, and I heard around the throne and the living creatures and the elders the voice of many angels, numbering myriads of myriads and thousands of thousands, saying with a loud voice, "Worthy is the Lamb who was slain, to receive power and wealth and wisdom and might and honor and glory and blessing!" (Revelation 5:11-12)

9. Have this mind among yourselves, which is yours in Christ Jesus, who though he was in the form of God, did not count equality with God a thing to be grasped, but emptied himself, taking the form of a servant, being born in the likeness of men. And being found in human form he humbled himself and became obedient unto death, even death on a cross. Therefore God has highly exalted him and bestowed on him the name which is above every name, that at the name of Jesus every knee should bow, in heaven and on earth and under the earth, and every tongue confess that Jesus Christ is Lord, to the glory of God the Father. (Philippians 2:5-11)

10. But we see Jesus, who for a little while was made lower than the angels, crowned with glory and honor because of the suffering of death, so that by the grace of God he might taste death for every one. For it was fitting that he, for whom and by whom all things exist, in bringing many sons to glory, should make the pioneer of their salvation perfect through suffering. (Hebrews 2:9-10)

11. Through him then let us continually offer up a sacrifice of praise to God, that is, the fruit of lips that acknowledge his name. Do not neglect to do good and to share what you have, for such sacrifices are pleasing to God. (Hebrews 13:15-16)

12. So put away all malice and all guile and insincerity and envy and all slander. Like newborn babes, long for the pure spiritual milk, that by it you may grow up to salvation; for you have tasted the kindness of the Lord. Come to him, to that living stone, rejected by men but in God's sight chosen and precious; and like living stones be yourselves built into a spiritual house, to be a holy priesthood, to offer spiritual sacrifices acceptable to God through Jesus Christ. (1 Peter 2:1-5)

13. So Jesus said to them, "Truly, truly, I say to you, unless you eat the flesh of the Son of man and drink his blood, you have no life in you; he who eats my flesh and drinks my blood has eternal life, and I will raise him up at the last day. For my flesh is food indeed, and my blood is drink indeed. He who eats my flesh and drinks my blood abides in me, and I in him. As the living Father sent me, and I live because of the Father, so he who eats me will live because of me. (John 6:53-57)

14. And I saw no temple in the city, for its temple is the Lord God Almighty and the Lamb. And the city has no need of sun or moon to shine upon it, for the glory of God is its light, and its lamp is the Lamb. (Revelation 21:22-23)

Invitations to the Table.

The invitation to the table is a brief statement addressed to the congregation asking them to participate in some appropriate manner. It can be a set of formal stage directions, explaining what is going to happen and asking the people to take part in designated ways. When understood in this way, the invitation will likely be worded something like this:

In our church the Lord's Supper is an act of worship open to all Christians. If you confess faith in Christ, are baptized and eligible to partake of communion in your own church, you are welcome at this table. This kind of statement can be printed in the bulletin, in which case it does not need to be announced.

The service is made stronger when the invitation is more a summons than stage directions. The tone can be gentle and inviting:

"Come to me, all who labor and are heavy-laden, and I will give you rest." (Matthew 11:28)

"Whoever, therefore, eats the bread and drinks the cup of the Lord in an unworthy manner will be guilty of profaning the body and blood of the Lord. Let a man examine himself and so eat of the bread and drink of the cup." (1Corinthians 11:27-28)

1. At this table we give thanks to God for the gifts he gives—life itself, the new life in Christ, and all of the supporting provisions that sustain us. Let us therefore prepare the table with our gifts, taken from life; and then by word and action praise the one who cares for us so richly.

2. We come to this table to remember Jesus Christ. He lived among us full of grace and truth. He was made perfect in suffering and has become the pioneer of our salvation. Let us therefore call out our praises and set the table with our thankofferings.

3. On the cross Jesus gave his life as a ransom for many, setting things right with God and inspiring persons to live the higher life. Let us prepare the table with elements of bread and wine which unite us with that sacrifice, reconcile us to God, and strengthen us for the Christian life.

4. Here at this table we are made to be friends of Jesus Christ and therefore of one another. Bring now your gifts, praying that they will become the instruments of this fellowship, carrying our spirits effectively to God who binds us together in Christian love.

5. At this table we break across the barriers of time and space and by God's Spirit are united with Jesus Christ. He who is separated from us by his divine splendor now lives in us and we in him. Come therefore to this holy table and enter into the mystery of our salvation.

Communion Meditations.

The communion meditation is a brief exposition of a theme related to the service of the Lord's Supper. Usually it is given early in the service very much as is the invitation. The two are distinguished from each other by their length and intent. The shorter of the two is the invitation which is a call to participate in the service, while the other is an interpretation of what the Lord's Supper means.

There are at least three conditions in which a communion meditation is suitable for a service of worship. The first is when the Lord's Supper is not preceeded by a sermon, or when the sermon does not lead the heart and mind to communion. The sermon, if rightly constructed, does open the mind and prepare the heart to act and speak at the table. Unfortunately, sermons do not always lead so well into the celebration of Christ's death upon the cross for our salvation. In these cases a communion meditation is probably necessary. Another condition when a meditation is appropriate is when the meaning of the Lord's Supper is to be high-lighted. In such times a brief interpretation of this sacrament can be of great help. A third condition is when the opening sentences of scripture need to be explained before they can function at their fullest.

There are dangers in using communion meditations. They can be too long, not well thought out, handled so as to interrupt the flow of the service, or be off the point.

1) The characteristic mode of the Christian life is thanksgiving. Christians are called to a life filled with positive qualities: faith, hope, and love, compassion, kindness, lowliness, meekness, and patience; and the list is just beginning. Shining through them all is thanksgiving. "And whatever you do, in word or deed," says the apostle, "do everything in the name of the Lord Jesus, giving thanks to God the Father through him" (Colossians 3:17).

Gratitude is our stance toward God because everything that we are and can be comes from him. He breathes into us the breath of life. He gives us this world of delight to enjoy and use. He supplies the powers of mind, body, and spirit which we need for our labors and recreations. Most important, he loves and forgives us, despite our disobedience. He promises to receive us back into his presence when this life ceases.

Gratitude is also our stance toward each other. In the life of the church we experience faith and encouragement, hope and inspiration, love and forgiveness. Because of this mutual ministry of nurture and support, each of us is helped to mature in the Christian life. How can we help but thank God always for each other?

Early Christians called their main service of worship "the eucharist," which translates into "the thanksgiving." With gifts

103

of bread and wine, and with their prayers, they proclaimed their thanks. Following their example we too come to the table with gifts and prayers—giving thanks to God the father through our Lord Jesus Christ.

2) The central focus of our Christian thanksgiving is Jesus Christ and the peace he established between creation and the Creator. We are to give thanks always—for life and all of its blessings. Yet the focal point of this thanksgiving, and the source of its constancy and abundance, is Jesus Christ in whom "all the fullness of God was pleased to dwell" (Colossians 1:19).

An ancient Christian hymn, which Paul incorporates into his letter to the Colossians (1:15-20), states this theme. In its first stanza the hymn celebrates Christ as the "image of the invisible God," and the agent by whom God created the universe. Its second stanza praises him as the one who has established reconciliation throughout the whole creation, "making peace by the blood of his cross." Paul then draws his conclusion: "As therefore you received Christ Jesus the Lord, so live in him, rooted and built up in him and established in the faith, just as you were taught, abounding in thanksgiving" (Colossians 2:6-7).

The Christ-centered character of our thanksgiving is portrayed in the church's celebration of the Lord's Supper. Here the bread and wine become the means whereby we share in the peace which Jesus brought about by his sacrifice. And we glimpse the creator God whom Jesus embodies, a God of justice and mercy, power and gentleness, majesty and lowliness.

This peace with all creation is not yet fully realized, but still we can rejoice. Christ has done his work and applied its benefits to us. Some day that cosmic peace will come. Therefore, let us give thanks.

3) Our thanksgiving to God and for each other takes the form of faithful, ardent, and joyful daily life. Thanksgiving is the major theme of the Christian life. Its central focus is Jesus Christ and the cosmic peace he established. Its form is life, for gratitude is clothed in ethics. Paul shows this to be the case in his letter to the Colossians when he joins a lyrical passage on thanksgiving to practical counsel about life in the home. It is as though he wanted us to understand that genuine thanks translates into such concrete realities as gentleness toward children and love between husband and wife.

This bond between thanksgiving and daily life explains why the Lord's Supper begins with the offering. What we really are doing is giving daily life—represented by bread, wine, and money—to God in gratitude for his gift of Jesus. We say thank you with all that we are, our hard work that overcomes laziness, our good appetites that stop short of gluttony, our gentleness in the face of cruelty, our efforts to achieve God's will despite frequent reverses.

This sacrament puts our life work in good perspective. By showing how seriously Christ Jesus took his work, to the point of shedding his blood, it invites us to take our life work with equal seriousness. We too are to live out our gratitude even to the point of death.

4) When Jesus met with his disciples for the last supper, he gave them a new meaning for a familiar act by saying whenever you do this remember me. Ceremonies with bread and wine were in common use among the Jews. On many occasions, and chiefly on the Passover, people would use a loaf and a cup as the focus for their prayers.

As host at the meal, Jesus took the bread and praised God for the gift of food. He then added something new to the familiar words. "Whenever you do this, remember me." After the meal he took the cup of blessing, again offering the expected prayer of thanksgiving and praise. A second time he stated the new meaning, "Whenever you do this, remember me."

Although they may not have understood him then, they soon were to find out what Jesus intended. They saw him imprisoned, tried, crucified, and buried. All of this they remembered when they broke the bread. And then they met him as risen Lord. This they remembered when they drank from the cup of blessing.

Obeying Jesus' instructions and following the example of early Christians, we too remember him. The loaf and cup connect us to Jesus' life and ministry. And in our prayers we retell the works of love and power by which he has given us life.

5) Remembrance at the Lord's Table is a sharing in the religious power of Christ's passion. On the cross Jesus poured out his blood for our salvation. By that act he reestablished peace between God and creation and created a new motivation for life among his followers. It was a powerful act.

But how does it span the years? How does the power of Calvary reach us now, these many generations later, these thousands of miles distant? We do not doubt the cosmic significant of Jesus' self-offering. Peace with God has been restored once and for all. But what of the experience of power? How are we to learn of that peace? How is the motivation to come to our lives?

The sacrament of the Lord's Supper is the means, for it links the human race and God. It repeatedly brings us to the cross on which he died. Coming to this table, we approach Calvary. Time is foreshortened, distance is erased, and we are made to participate in our Lord's passion and victory. "Here, O my Lord, I see thee face to face." That is what it means to remember Jesus.

6) Remembrance at the Lord's Table not only connects us to the past but it projects us toward the future. Anticipation of what is to come is very much like the remembering of what has been. In both cases our experience of time is altered so that we live simultaneously in two times—the "right now" and the "not right now."

The Lord's Supper obviously connects us to the events long ago when our Christian faith was brought into being. It also connects us to the Christian vision of creation brought to its fulfillment, when sin is destroyed and suffering is overcome, when age-old animosities are transcended and hopes for community are realized.

Under the pressures of daily life, this vision fades and its driving power weakens. That is why we need to experience that longed for future while we still are bound by the realities of this present time. Therefore we come to the Holy Table, to be caught up with the future, with the new heaven and new earth which God promises to create and let us enjoy. For this reason we eat and drink together in peace and joy, sharing for a moment of time the delights of the new age. Strengthened by that vision, we can continue our work in the "right now."

7) A meal is a powerful event, providing the substance from which life is built and binding us effectively both to the divine and to each other. Aware of this potency in a meal, Paul advises us to eat and drink with care. Our breaking of bread, he says, can put us in communion with God or with the demons, with the transcendent source of good or with the transcendent powers of evil. His first audience understood him easily because they were surrounded by ceremonial meals of several religions. From their own experience they knew this connection between food and faith.

In our more secular age the religious meaning of meals is less evident, yet still real. The form and substance of a meal, and the circumstances in which it is eaten and drunk, connect us with power. Sometimes that power erodes our confidence and stability, breaking down character and personality. It puts us in touch with demonic powers that destroy.

Meals connect us to power that creates and sustains; and foremost among them is the Lord's Supper. We are brought to the cross which links heaven and earth, bringing about the exchange of spirit between us and God. Our spirits of praise and penitence are lifted up to him; his Holy Spirit of mercy and vitality is given to us.

Therefore, let us approach this table with due attention to its potency. Here we eat and drink with God.

8) Our fellowship is with the Father and with his Son Jesus Christ. John makes this claim in his epistle addressed to Christians everywhere. We want to believe him: that persons today can enjoy the companionship of Jesus Christ. He is portrayed in the gospels as forceful, sensitive, good in conversation, trustworthy, the kind of person we want to be with. Even more, he carries with him the powerful presence of God so that seeing him is seeing God himself.

Yet how can we enjoy this companionship? His life among us was long ago and far away. And now he has returned to his father's house from which we are denied entrance while bound to this world of time and space.

The Lord's Supper becomes a means for us to be brought into contact with him. It breaks across the barriers of time so that we live briefly in that ancient land where Jesus lived his manhood. We are made to be members of the crowd whom he fed with loaves and fish, and with the word of life. This table breaks across the barriers of space so that we are momentarily united with thousands of thousands at the throne of God crying "worthy is the Lamb" (Revelation 5:12).

Like Thomas we want to be close enough to touch his hands and feet, but that degree of intimacy is denied us. Instead, we have this meal of remembrance and hope whose host is Jesus Christ, man of Nazareth and heavenly friend. Let us rejoice, for here we do have fellowship—with God our Father and with his Son Jesus Christ.

9) In this banquet hall we are joined with an immense crowd of Christians who share our faith in Christ and our joy in the life to which he calls us. Peter, Stephen, Lydia, and Paul are seated at a table near the front. Not far away are Justin and Augustine. At

other tables Luther, Edwards, Schweitzer, and countless other Christians have joined the fellowship. For Jesus has saved us "from every tribe and tongue and people and nation" (Revelation 5:9). This is our common table where we meet him and each other.

This church where today we spread the table is but an alcove of the banquet hall. Here we are permitted to enjoy our own way of life, using our language, our forms of bread and wine, our ceremonies and customs. Elsewhere others enjoy the same freedom to be themselves.

But the unity is greater than the differences. For in every room Christ is himself the host; and on every table the bread we break becomes for us his body and the cup his blood of the covenant poured out for the forgiveness of sins.

Let us therefore join hands with our brothers and sisters everywhere. Although we speak different languages and perform gestures unfamiliar to each other, we are joined in a festive meal that all enjoy. It is the joyous feast of the people of God.

10) The communion table is a place where Christians meet each other. This place is one of the focal points of worship, a major reason for our coming together, and an act in which we regularly join in common effort.

It is a meeting place in a more significant way. This ceremony with bread and wine expresses the foundation of our corporate life. We assemble in the house of worship not because of friendliness and charm, but because Jesus gave his life for us and we in turn have given our lives to him.

This double gift is embodied in the elements on the table which connect us to his redeeming sacrifice and express our responding sacrifice of praise and thanksgiving. It scarcely matters that we are so different from one another in manner of life and attitudes toward the powers of this world.

Here we are united in faith and commitment. At this table we really meet each other.

11) The meaning of Jesus' life and work is often summed up in language drawn from the Hebrew practice of sacrifice. Following the feeding of the 5,000 Jesus explained the deeper significance of the act by saying: "For my flesh is food indeed, and my blood is drink indeed. He who eats my flesh and drinks my blood abides in me, and I in him" (John 6:55-56). The epistle to the Hebrews can be described as one long sermon in which the practice of animal sacrifice is used as the metaphor to explain Jesus. He is

described both as priest who performs the sacrifice and as the victim whose blood is shed. The writer exclaims that Jesus "has appeared once for all at the end of the age to put away sin by the sacrifice of himself" (Hebrews 9:26).

If this talk of sacrifice sounds strange to us, it may be because we use the term more often in patriotic discourse than in religious. We do understand what it means, that someone gives his or her life for the sake of others.

Although Jesus' sacrifice occurred long ago, its religious power continues to operate. At this table we come into contact. This bread . . . my body given for you. This wine . . . my blood shed for you. His self-offering done once for all accomplishes its intention now and for us. He who once *made* atonement for the sins of the world now *makes* it for you and me.

12) When Jesus offered himself as a sacrifice for sin, he released new power for daily life. He overcame sin and reestablished peace between God and his creation. The sin which weighed us down would do so no longer. The alienation from God which had distorted our every effort would no longer do that evil work.

How unbelieving we are. Although free to live as God wants us to, we seem paralyzed by uncertainty. For that reason the author of the epistle to the Hebrews closes his teaching about Jesus' sacrifice with an exhortation. Since you have been cleansed from sin, he says, "stir up one another to love and good works, not neglecting to meet together. . . ." (Hebrews 10:24, 25).

That same message comes to us at the table of the Lord. The bread and wine, Christ's body and blood, renew in us his saving act. They tell us that sin and its power over us have been overcome. They encourage us to live accordingly—free, courageous, joyful, aggressively good. When we take that advice, the results surprise us. We discover what Paul had learned, that we can do all things through Christ who strengthens us.

The Offering

In this book I am showing how the offering is directly connected to the feast of joy. It is the setting of the communion table. When that is the case one invitation can be extended in which people are invited to participate in the offering and in communion. The communion meditation can then cover the offering too; the communion prayer becomes also the offertory prayer. A service set up this way moves quickly and directly through its several parts: approach to the offering/communion, offering, communion prayer, breaking of bread, communion.

In some services, however, the offering is not so closely interwoven with the communion. The separation means that there is a need for materials designed specifically for the offering as giving money to the church, and in this section I am providing examples. Offertory words may be sentences of scripture read without comment, or they can be developed to include an invitation to give and a meditation upon the meaning of the act. When the offering is a separate element in the service, it will usually include a dedicatory prayer. A logical arrangement of the parts when the offertory deals strictly with money is: invitation, sentences of scripture or meditation, collecting the gifts, ceremonial presentation of the gifts, and dedicatory prayer.

Scripture Sentences

1. This is the thing which the Lord has commanded. Take from among you an offering to the Lord; whoever is of a generous heart, let him bring the Lord's offering." (Exodus 35:4b-5a)

2. Offer to God a sacrifice of thanksgiving, and pay your vows to the most High." (Psalm 50:14)

3. With a free-will offering I will sacrifice to thee; I will give thanks to thy name, O Lord, for it is good." (Psalm 54:6)

4. Honor and majesty are before him;
     strength and beauty are in his sanctuary.
   Ascribe to the Lord, O families of the peoples,
     ascribe to the Lord glory and strength!
   Ascribe to the Lord the glory due his name;
     bring an offering, and come into his courts! (Psalm 96:6-8)

5. What shall I render to the Lord
     for all his bounty to me?
   I will lift up the cup of salvation
     and call on the name of the Lord,
   I will pay my vows to the Lord
     in the presence of all his people. (Psalm 116:12-14)

6. Do not lay up for yourselves treasures on earth, where moth and rust consume and where thieves break in and steal, but lay up for yourselves treasures in heaven, where neither moth nor rust consumes and where thieves do not break in and steal; for where your treasure is, there will your heart be also. (Matthew 6:19-21)

7. The Lord our God, the Lord is one; and you shall love the Lord your God with all your heart, and with all your soul, and with all your mind, and with all your strength. (Mark 12:29-30)

8. And he sat down opposite the treasury, and watched the multitude putting money into the treasury. Many rich people put in large sums. And a poor widow came, and put in two copper coins, which make a penny. And he called his disciples to him, and said to them, "Truly, I say to you, this poor widow has put in more than all those who are contributing to the treasury. For they all contributed out of their abundance; but she out of her poverty has put in everything she had, her whole living." (Mark 12:41-44)

9. And he said to all, "If any man would come after me, let him deny himself and take up his cross daily and follow me." (Luke 9:23)

10. Sell your possessions, and give alms; provide yourselves with purses that do not grow old, with a treasure in the heavens that does not fail, where no thief approaches and no moth destroys. For where your treasure is, there will your heart be also. (Luke 12:33-34)

11. Now as you excel in everything—in faith, in utterance, in knowledge, in all earnestness, and in your love for us—see that you excel in this gracious work also. (2 Corinthians 8:7)

12. Each of you must do as he has made up his mind, not reluctantly or under compulsion, for God loves a cheerful giver. (2 Corinthians 9:7)

13. Do not neglect to do good and to share what you have, for such sacrifices are pleasing to God. (Hebrews 13:16)

14. As each has received a gift, employ it for one another, as good stewards of God's varied grace. (1 Peter 4:10)

15. If any man has the world's goods and sees his brother in need, yet closes his heart against him, how does God's love abide in him? Little children, let us not love in word or speech but in deed and in truth. (1 John 3:17-18)

Invitations to the Offering

1) The money which we give to Christ's church is a dramatic sign of an even costlier gift, our own selves returned to God in gratitude for his goodness. This greater gift is presented to him in daily life: in our work and play, in our private reflections and public actions. Yet in church we also give the sign in order to keep clear what all of the rest means. When we bring these offerings to God, we remind ourselves and testify to the world that all of life belongs to him.

2) When we bring a portion of our income to the church we throw our weight and influence on the side of things in which we believe. The church and its institutions deserve to live. But their support does not come from taxes or general community funds. They exist, and languish or flourish, because you and I give our money, and that in substantial amounts. Every offering is a referendum for the church's future. Today, let's vote aye.

3) By bringing our gifts to the church we, in a small way, follow the example of Jesus who said that it is more blessed to give than to receive. Most of us are not called upon to give up family and friends, job and security to be like him. But we are expected to use all of these possessions as a trust. They are to be made serviceable to others. The gifts we bring today are a pledge that this is what we intend to do: to be blessed by our giving rather than by our getting.

4) When we bring an offering to the church we express our solidarity with those who hunger and are heavy laden, both here and around the world. While we may not be ready to sell all that we have and give it to the poor, we are willing to share some of our abundance with those around us. Let the gesture be an eloquent one.

5) Our gifts to God through his church are a pledge that we want the kingdoms of this world to become the kingdom of our Lord and Savior Jesus Christ. Money bears the mark of the rulers of this earth. We take the sign of their sovereignty and say that, as much as we are able, we will turn them over to the higher rule of Christ himself. It was he who said: "render to Caesar the things that are Caesar's and to God the things that are God's." (Matthew 22:21)

113

Offertory Prayers

1) Creator God: You have given us the life we live, and now in gratitude we pledge ourselves to your service. Accept this money that we bring to your church as a sign of our intentions to give all of life to you. In Jesus' name. Amen.

2) O God: You have given us the church as a preview of your kingdom where love and justice will rule. In gratitude we bring our offerings to show that we are on your side. Through Christ our Lord. Amen.

3) With this offering, Father of us all, we commit ourselves to follow the example of our Lord Jesus Christ who said that it is more blessed to give than to receive. Help us to make good on our intention. In his name we pray. Amen.

4) Eternal God: We hear the cries of the world groaning in travail, waiting for its redemption. With these gifts of money brought to your church, we intend to show our solidarity with all who suffer. Let our gifts ease the pain and renew hope. We pray through Jesus Christ. Amen.

5) King of the universe: You have placed us in nations under the rule of mortals like ourselves. We bring these gifts to your church as a sign that our higher allegiance is to you. Help us, we pray, to work so that the rulers of this world will subject their wills to yours. In the name of Jesus Christ. Amen.

The Communion Prayer

The communion prayer brings all of the service into focus. It praises God for his glory and mercy, for his gift of life in Jesus Christ, and for his life-giving Spirit. In this prayer leaders of the congregation ask God's help for all Christians who want to respond to him in loving service.

In the free tradition to whom this manual is addressed the prayer is short, prepared new for each occasion, and free to express the widely varying sentiments of the congregation. This tradition presupposes that the congregation is already united with the living Christ and that the prayer is the conversation that results. Ordinarily the prayer mentions the bread and wine and suggests a relationship between these elements and Christ's body and blood given for us. Yet this tradition forces no obligations upon the prayer, either of form or of theological content.

The prayers on the following pages follow the pattern discussed in chapter five, "Offering the Communion Prayer": thanksgiving, remembrance, calling upon the Holy Spirit, rededication of life to his service. In many congregations the custom is that two such prayers are offered, one for the loaf and one for the cup. In other congregations only one communion prayer is offered. The references to bread and wine in the following prayers will have to be adapted to the circumstances.

1. Creator of all that is, we praise you:
>   For your own self, beautiful and filled with light;
>   For your works, incredibly varied and fruitful;
>   For life itself and consciousness with which to enjoy it.
> Redeemer of all creation groaning in travail, we praise you:
>   For your justice that holds us to the standard that all
>   things created are good;
>   For your mercy that forgives and renews us when we fall
>   short;
>   For your promise that all things will be made new.
> Most of all we praise you for Jesus Christ:
>   Through him you created the world;
>   By his life and ministry you showed us your nature;
>   Because of his suffering and death you saved us;
>   By his resurrection you gave us power to live.
> We bring you these gifts of bread and wine to be a sign of our gratitude, O God, for all that you are and have done for us in Jesus Christ.
> As we eat the bread and drink from the cup of salvation, renew in us the presence of your Holy Spirit.
>   Cleanse us from sin.
>   Restore us to new life.
> And then send us into the world as signs of your creativity and agents of the redemption that you are bringing.
>   Through Christ we pray. Amen.

2. We come to this table, Holy Father, bewildered and uncertain, hoping
>   to find answers to the mystery of life.

So much happens to us that we can neither understand nor control:
    Sickness that weakens body and mind;
    Frustration of our efforts and hopes;

    The breaking apart of communities to which we belong;
    The battle within that leads us to do the things we don't
        want to do and fail to achieve our real intentions.
We praise you that in this sacrament of bread and wine, by which
    you unite us with Jesus Christ, there is the resolution of
        our distress.
    He identified himself with our weakness, yet without
        sin.
    He faced all the powers that weaken and destroy, yet
        without giving in.
    He rose from the dead and ever lives, making interces-
        sion for us.
As we share this meal of remembrance, O God, apply to us again
    Christ's saving work.
Send us the Holy Spirit which he promised so that we can
    leave this house confident and filled with hope.
Assist us, thus strengthened, to use these powers to help others
    find abundant life in Jesus Christ.
    In his name we pray. Amen.

3. Lord, for the signs of your powerful and surprising presence
    we give you thanks:
        The steady coming and going of the seasons;
        The constant productivity of the earth;
        The dependable cycle of life;
        The irrepressibility of love and forgiveness in the face of
            evil.
Even more we thank you for Jesus Christ who fully expressed
your majesty and immediacy.
At this table, set with our gifts of gratitude, we remember
him:
        His gentle and quiet life;
        His charismatic presence;
        His singular sense of divine vocation;

His faithfulness against all odds.
And we praise you that by his sacrifice he showed us your own nature clearly and powerfully.
By your Holy Spirit:
> Open our eyes that we may see you face to face;
> Enliven our bodies that we may touch and handle things unseen;
> Unlock our wills that we may accomplish the work you
give us to do.
In the name of Jesus Christ. Amen.

4. Author of life:
For every chapter in the book you have written we give you thanks:
> The seven days of creation when all was good;
> The age of the patriarchs when your mercy toward sinners was
> stronger than your wrath over their sin;
> The times of the prophets when courageous persons dared violence and loneliness
> to speak your words of justice and forgiveness.
Most of all we praise you for Jesus Christ, who in the fullness of time came to save us from our sins.
> In his life he told us of your will;
> In his death he showed us your love;
> In his resurrection he demonstrated your power.
All of this we remember with bread and wine, the sacrament of his body and blood poured out for us.
With these gifts, representing our life and labor, we also praise you.
Take us and use us to write a new chapter in your book of life,
> in which injustice is put down and your way made known over all the earth.
Through Jesus Christ our Lord. Amen.

5. Your greatness, God, exceeds our knowledge.
You reveal wonders and do things that we cannot understand.
> To the snow you say "fall on the earth."
> You breathe and the ice is there.
> The surface of the waters freezes over.

Because you are clothed in such fearful splendor we hold you in awe.
But because of Jesus we love you also.
By his life and death, which we celebrate with this bread and cup,
he showed us that you temper justice with mercy,
power with gentleness,
granduer with love.
Therefore we dare to approach you despite your awesome greatness.
With his blood cover our sin, as with the snow you cover the earth.
Drive away the impurities of heart and life, as with your icy breath you purify the earth.
Stir up within us the fire of your Holy Spirit so that we can endure the rigors of life's assaults.
Help us to go from this house of prayer proclaiming your glory in every place and sharing life with those around us.
Through Christ we pray. Amen.

6. God of glory and majesty,
whose power is so great that we cannot bear it,
whose presence so awesome we are struck dumb,
whose radiance so brilliant that our eyes are blinded:
We thank you for finding ways of making yourself known:
in fire and cloud and light,
in the ancient law delivered upon the mountain,
in the special history of the Hebrews long ago.
Especially do we thank you for Jesus, made in your image,
who has come to live among us to show us what you are really like.
Here at this table, by candle's fire, and bread and wine, our eyes are opened.
Seeing Jesus we see you again and are satisfied.
Forgive us our fear and forgetfulness and faulty vision.
And send us your Holy Spirit so that we who see you again will live faithfully and well, with lives marked by justice, mercy, and good faith.
In the name of Christ. Amen.

7. God of steadfast love, we praise you for your constancy:
In creation ever being renewed you pour out your own heart of beauty and joy.
In providential care you show your continuing concern

119

for the world you made.
In prophets and saints you reveal your will.
In Jesus Christ our Lord you show how much you care
for us.
In these and all your acts you reveal your love which persists
regardless of what we do.
Especially do we thank you for Jesus Christ in whose life and
death and resurrection from the grave you show your
steadfast love fully and completely.
With this bread and wine we remember him and offer you
honor and praise.
By your Holy Spirit kindle in our hearts a love like yours so
that we, like Jesus, can give ourselves in lives of loving
service.
In the name of Christ. Amen.

8. Eternal God: In the scriptures it says
that you teach your people how to walk,
that you correct them,
and comfort them,
that you give them what they need even before they ask
for it.
For these expressions of your fatherly love we give you thanks.
Even more we praise you for sharing your son with us.
By his life and ministry,
his suffering and death,
and his resurrection from the dead,
he has strengthened the ties that bind us to you.
As we share this meal together, renew our beloved family of
memory and hope,
with you as father and Jesus our older brother,
and with all of us here gathered brothers and sisters.
We pray in Christ's name. Amen.

9. Dear Father:
Once again your Word has called us to the foot of the cross
where Jesus, strong of body and clear of mind,
gave up his life for us.
And now you invite us, when we eat this bread and drink
from the cup of blessing, to receive again the benefits of
his passion:
forgiveness, a new beginning for life, and the indwelling
power of the Holy Spirit to achieve that life.
For these gifts we praise you.

At this table of remembrance we promise once again to follow
  our Lord's example, using our new life to help others
  come to a fuller knowledge of Jesus and his steadfast
  love.
In his name we pray. Amen.

10. Eternal God, Father of lights, we adore you.
When the world was first begun you placed lamps in the
      heavens,
  the sun to rule by day,
  the moon and stars by night.
Through all the ages since you have given us these sources of
necessity and delight:
  warming our bodies,
  cheering our spirits,
  causing the earth to bring forth its green growth and life.
For the sun of creation that shines so brilliantly in its
aethereal sky, we give you thanks.
Even more we praise you for the Son of Righteousness whom
you raised from the dead on Easter day.
  By his words and acts of power he revealed your will.
  By his suffering and death he showed your steadfast love.
  By his rising again he reflected your glory and majesty,
      giving light to those who live in darkness.
All glory be to you, O God.
When we eat this bread and drink this wine, tear the clouds
away from our eyes so that we can behold his brightness.
And then fill us with your Holy Spirit so that we will be
empowered to grow and flower in this world where you have
planted us.
In the name of Christ we pray. Amen.

14

Breaking of Bread and
the Distribution

The breaking of bread can be an action without words or explanation. In such instances it needs to be done at a deliberate pace and so that people can see and hear. A small loaf of bread, such as a dinner roll, might be used. Or the breaking might be accompanied by music sung by the choir, perhaps one verse of a hymn which states one of the meanings of communion. Probably the most common practice is for the leader to accompany the breaking of bread with sentences that express the meaning of the service. This is one place where the words of institution often are used. When saying that Jesus took bread, the leader picks up the loaf, breaking it when that point is reached in the narration. The cup can also be lifted up, or the trays touched, during the latter part of the words of institution.

Other words can also be used, and a small selection follows.

1.   *As the minister breaks the bread:*
   The bread which we break,
   is it not a participation in the body of Christ?
        As the minister lifts the cup:
   The cup of blessing which we bless,
   is it not a participation in the blood of Christ?
        The Congregation:
   Unite us to you and to one another, O Lord,
   as we all partake of the one loaf.
        Or:
   As you did to the disciples of old, O Lord,
   make yourself known to us in the breaking of bread.

2. Jesus, Lamb of God:
        have mercy on us.
   Jesus, bearer of our sins:
        have mercy on us.
   Jesus, redeemer of the world:
        give us your peace.

3. *Minister*   Alleluia. Christ our Passover
                     is sacrificed for us.
   People   Therefore let us keep the feast. Alleluia.
   Minister   Blessed is he who comes in the name of the Lord.
   People   Hosanna in the highest.
   Minister   The gifts of God for the people of God.
                     (An Order of Worship, p. 32)

The Conclusion

Just as the approach is a way of starting things off neatly and gracefully, so the conclusion brings communion to a close. It should be done quickly. The form of the conclusion will depend in part on the manner of distribution. When the partaking has been in unison, there will be a sentence said by the leader which becomes a signal to partake together and a way of summing up the service. When persons partake as the trays are passed, there still can be a sentence after all have finished. Either in addition to the sentence, or in place of it, the leader can offer a brief prayer. If this is done, it ordinarily is a final word of thanksgiving for the privilege of the Feast of Joy. In addition to the suggestions above, the communion hymn can serve as frame, bringing the service to a close as well as opening it up.

One beautiful closing to the service is the ancient Christian song formed out of the prayer offered by Simeon after he had seen the baby Jesus (Luke 2:29-32). It can be said by the leader, sung by the choir or congregation, or recited in unison. The text, in ecumenical translation from the Greek, follows.

Lord, now you let your servant go in peace;
your word has been fulfilled.
My own eyes have seen the salvation
which you have prepared in the sight of every people:
a light to reveal you to the nations
and the glory of your people Israel.

Scripture Sentences for Unison Partaking of Communion

1. Whoever seeks to gain his life will lose it, but whoever loses his life will preserve it. (Luke 17:33)

2. And the Word became flesh and dwelt among us, full of grace and truth; we have beheld his glory, glory as of the only Son from the Father. (John 1:14)

3. Behold the Lamb of God, who takes away the sin of the world. (John 1:29)

4. For God so loved the world that he gave his only Son, that whoever believes in him should not perish but have eternal life. (John 3:16)

5. But whoever drinks of the water that I shall give him will never thirst; the water that I shall give him will become in him a spring of water welling up to eternal life. (John 4:14)

6. Do not labor for the food which perishes, but for the food which endures to eternal life, which the Son of man will give to you; for on him has God the Father set his seal. (John 6:27)

7. I am the bread of life; he who comes to me shall not hunger, and he who believes in me shall never thirst. (John 6:35)

8. I am the living bread which came down from heaven; if any one eats of this bread, he will live for ever; and the bread which I shall give for the life of the world is my flesh. (John 6:51)

9. He who loves his life loses it, and he who hates his life in this

world will keep it for eternal life. (John 12:25)

10. So whether you eat or drink, or whatever you do, do all to the glory of God. (1 Corinthians 10:31)

11. For as often as you eat this bread and drink the cup, you proclaim the Lord's death until he comes. (1 Corinthians 11:26)

12. But now in Christ Jesus you who once were far off have been brought near in the blood of Christ. (Ephesians 2:13)

13. Rejoice in the Lord always; again I will say, Rejoice. (Ephesians 4:4)

14. For in him all the fullness of God was pleased to dwell, and through him to reconcile to himself all things, whether on earth or in heaven, making peace by the blood of his cross. (Colossians 1:19-20)

15. Although he was a Son, he learned obedience through what he suffered; and being made perfect he became the source of eternal salvation to all who obey him. (Hebrews 5:8-9)

Prayers at the Close of Communion

1. For this feast of joy we give you thanks, O God. Help us share the delight of the Christian life with those we meet in the days ahead. Through Jesus Christ our Lord. Amen.

2. You have blessed us, good Father, with the bread of life. Show us how to use the strength it gives as we go about our daily work. Through Christ our Lord. Amen.

3. Eternal God, at this table you have given us a new measure of your Holy Spirit. By this gift lead and empower us. In the name of Jesus Christ. Amen.

4. With this bread and wine, O God, you have renewed our experience of Christ's sacrifice. Cleansed by his blood, we now pledge to follow his example of sacrificial service to those around us. In his name. Amen.

5. In this joyous meal, dear God, you have united us with Christ Jesus and with one another. Help us to extend this new community into all the world. In his name we pray. Amen.